D1577577

,

SILVER LININGS

Jess Impiazzi

Hashtag PRESS

Published in Great Britain by Hashtag Press 2020

A CIP catalogue for this book is available from the British Library.

ISBN 978-1-9162864-7-4

Typeset in Garamond Classic 11.5/14.5 by Blaze Typesetting

Printed and bound in Great Britain by Clays Ltd, Elcograf S.p.A.

Hashtag PRESS

HASHTAG PRESS BOOKS
Hashtag Press Ltd
Kent, England, United Kingdom
Email: info@hashtagpress.co.uk
Website: www.hashtagpress.co.uk
Twitter: @hashtag_press

I dedicate this book to all of you who may have suffered in silence, to those who have the light inside them but are struggling to notice. To those whose hearts have been broken and those who must remember their worth. Once you remember that, your world will change.
Never forget the power of you!

Acknowledgements

I am so full of love and gratitude for every single person who has walked beside me on my journey, each and every one of you have given me lessons and propelled me on to such huge personal growth. I would not have been able to get here without you.

To my Mum for showing me that, even in darkness, you can find the light.

To my forever friends and family for being there when my world was uncertain and rocky. I love you dearly for seeing the light in me when I could not see it in myself.

I realise now that we are all one, the power of love, compassion and understanding can pull us out of any hardship, and my promise to the world is to help others find that too.

I'd like to thank my publishers, Abiola and Helen at Hashtag Press, for taking on my first book and my agents Madeline and Greg at WGM Literacy, for guiding me through the process.

Introduction

If you go on my social media, you will see a young woman, always smiling and having a good time. But I have had some tough moments in my life, starting in childhood. Lots of terrible things happened and I witnessed a horrible amount of domestic violence in my home. Acting and writing were my escape from the chaos. Throughout my life three things have occupied my attention and distracted me without fail: making up stories, daydreaming and acting.

My childhood was, in parts, quite traumatic, which created self-confidence issues. I was a chatty little thing, especially to adults and my mum's friends, but I would often get shy in front of people from my peer group and I would easily blush. I was always more confident and comfortable around adults.

I knew from a young age that I wanted to be on stage and to perform and write. So in my early teens, aged around fourteen, I left my local school in Haslemere in Surrey to join the Italia Conti Academy of Theatre Arts. I found the confidence to be myself. It was practically sink or swim at theatre school and I decided to swim.

By Year Eleven, I was so much happier in myself. I think theatre school taught me how to be a kid again. When I moved school, I lived with my nan and grandad, so I had a much calmer home life there. I'd come home and prance around the front room, showing my grandparents everything I'd learnt at school.

They'd say, "Oh, it's so wonderful, darling!" and give me a round of applause. It is still my favourite sound.

Even more than dancing, though, was my love of acting. I wanted to be an actor. I lost my confidence when I left acting school to help my mum when she suddenly went blind. I didn't realise at the time how big an impact that decision had on me. I'd given up everything I'd worked for. It didn't matter, because it was tiny compared to what my mum was going through and I was so happy to be in a position to help her. I thought my chances of being a dancer or an actor were over, which was why I was so grateful that I had what I saw as a second chance after being cast by MTV on *Ex on the Beach*. It felt as if I had being given another opportunity.

I knew reality TV wasn't acting, and I was nervous about it causing problems for me getting acting work in the future, but I was desperate to move forward. I needed to feel I was worth something. Everything collapsed around me when I left school and life hadn't got much better. MTV felt like a chance to at least be in front of a camera.

The first time I went on that show I had the time of my life. I made a few stupid choices, things that I can't take back, but I've grown through it all. It helped me to build a social media platform and get more recognition. At first, I wasn't great with being recognised. I behaved like a total idiot in front of the paparazzi, as I thought that was how I was "supposed" to behave. I didn't know who I was any more, so I became what I thought a reality/glamour girl was supposed to be. I look back now and cringe. We can't change the past, but we can learn from it, and I guess that's the main thing. There's always a silver lining.

CHAPTER ONE

When Your Mum Goes Blind

When the professors of the famous Moorfields Eye Hospital in London told us that my mum was losing her eyesight and would have to adjust to life as a blind person, we couldn't quite believe it. How was this possible? What did it mean for her future? Our future?

We grew up watching Mum suffer from poor eyesight and she was registered visually impaired for as long as I remember. In those days we had to walk (rather than her drive us) everywhere, which was great; it kept us very fit! Other than that, I can assure you that she lived life to the full. She loved a party and in fact that hasn't changed. She was always so beautiful and that hasn't changed either. Always lapping up attention. So this bombshell from the professors almost felt like nonsense.

She was born with a rare genetic disorder called Uveal effusion syndrome. Both parents have to carry this specific gene for their child to have eye issues, and my nan and grandad were both carriers. The scientific definition is complex and it is a rare syndrome making it even more confusing. In simple terms though, a fluid was building up behind my mum's eye, causing the retina to die, ultimately producing sight loss.

Mum was on holiday with my stepdad Jim when she started to lose her sight. She noticed one eye wasn't right. Once she was back home, she went to hospital to find out what was going on. Within two weeks she was completely blind in one eye and after eighteen months she had lost sight in both. None of us could believe it was happening. I just thought she would get better. I kept making my little wishes that things would change.

It was hard for us, as a family, to adapt to what was happening her. We needed to figure out our new roles. It was only my stepdad and myself at home. I would return from college in the evenings and find that she was still on the sofa where she'd been when I had left earlier that day.

I'd say, "Mum, you haven't moved all day!"

She was scared to get up. It broke my heart to see. I wanted to fix it more than anything, but it was completely out of our control. It's hard to see someone you love in pain. You want to do all you can to make everything better but I felt hopeless.

That's when I knew what I had to do. I dropped out of my theatre school, Italia Conti. When your mum goes blind you have to decide how to help her. You have to re-evaluate everything in your life. You don't realise how hard it will be. If she put a cup down and forgot about it, she wouldn't know where it was and would have to ask for help. You couldn't say, "It's there," because she didn't know where "there" was any more. She was sinking into a deep depression.

What were we going to do? How were we going to get through this?

I clearly remember Mum's doctor, Professor Bird, at Moorfields Eye Hospital in London. I really liked him. He was an older gentleman with white hair; I thought of him as a wise old owl.

When my brother and I were quite young we would regularly travel with Mum up to Moorfields. Mum has been visiting that hospital regularly since she was a baby. When we were little, my brother and I were tested to see if we carried the gene too. The doctor put drops in our eyes to dilate our pupils. I couldn't see for about an hour afterwards and everything was blurry. It was scary. I guess we were getting a small taste of what Mum had been through since she was born.

I knew we had to do something to help Mum lead a normal life once her sight had gone, and help her learn how to adapt as a blind person. We started going to Braille class. I'd pick up three elderly ladies and drive them with Mum every week in the Ford Ka my nan bought me. Two were visually impaired; one was blind. They'd get into my tiny car and I'd drive them all over the place.

They had been dealing with sight problems longer than my mum so in a way they were like her mentors. One of the ladies, Margaret, had this awful condition where her vision would be constantly moving, so everything was blurred. Mum and I used to go and visit her for a cup of tea. We liked the company and we learned a lot from her. We found her to be an inspiration. She would go about her life without complaint; she got such joy from making her own jams and we would buy them off her. She showed us that no matter the disability you can still live, as long as you're doing things that make your heart sing. Jam making was Margaret's and, boy, did she make good jam!

Mum wasn't the same after losing her sight, but you're not going to be, are you? You've got to adapt to a brand new world.

We don't realise how much we do in life without appreciating our sight. It was difficult for her to come to terms with not being able to do things for herself.

There are so many things we take for granted: being able to see, smell, hear and taste. Right now I'm sitting at my kitchen table with my laptop open, every few minutes glancing at my phone to see if anyone's texted me, and then I gaze out the window. I check what time it is on the big clock on the wall. Those of us who do not live in darkness rarely think how lucky we are.

I don't know where my mum would be without Kasey: my mum's first-ever guide dog. She has been a life-changer. The Guide Dogs for the Blind Association really are incredible. The amazing dogs have given Mum, and so many others just like her, their freedom and independence back and I cannot ever thank them enough.

I remember when Mum was doing her white stick training. At first she hated it. When she went out with her stick she didn't feel safe.

She said to her trainer, "I hate this cane; I feel so disabled."

"Imagine if you didn't have that white stick. How disabled would you feel then?" her trainer replied.

That really stuck with her. She realised this was her life now. You can't keep wishing for things to be how they used to be. You have to accept the new reality. It's hard. There are so many idiots around. Once we were out with her white stick and a van drove past and these blokes shouted, "How many fingers am I holding up?"

Luckily they drove off, otherwise they'd have seen which finger I was holding up.

When she was quite new with her stick, Mum walked into a scaffolding truck that was parked across the pavement. It nearly took her face off. It gave her a big black eye. She was lucky it wasn't so much worse.

This happened all the time. People aren't aware of the dangers they are causing. The streets are so full of hazards, even if you have fully adapted to not being able to see, or for people in wheelchairs or with any other disabilities. That's why I want to raise awareness for blind people. To ensure people pay more attention to their careless actions, which cause day-to-day problems for people with disabilities.

Getting a guide dog was the best thing that could have possibly happened. It meant that Mum wasn't relying on any of us to take her to the shops as Kasey learnt the route. Going to the shop with Kasey helped build up Mum's confidence.

Guide dogs really are magical. They're able to prevent you from doing things like walking into scaffolding poles that are hanging out of irresponsibly-parked vans on the curb! It was so beautiful watching Mum and Kasey get to know each other. Mum could now do things by herself again.

Being blind is like moving into a new town. You have to learn to navigate your way around.

One time we were walking to the train station and there was a guy on a scooter—an adult—and we wanted to walk past him as he was stationary and blocking our path, but he just froze. Mum was holding my arm and he could see she was blind and I was thinking, *You're in our way! Move!* I had to guide her around him.

Mum could tell I was annoyed and said, "Jess, what's going on?"

I said, "It's just a man, confused, who doesn't know what to do!" and Mum and I burst out laughing.

We were thinking, *You can see so just move!*

Mum told me a story about when she went on a train by herself, which still makes my blood boil. To catch a train alone, she would usually book travel assistance and an employee of the travel service would put her safely on a carriage and then at the destination another would help her. However, this particular time, the assistance was late and Mum just spoke up as she heard someone pass her.

"Excuse me, I'm blind, would you be able to help me off the train?"

It would literally take thirty seconds to help a blind person off the train with you but this vile woman said, "No," and walked off.

This sort of behaviour makes me so mad. It's disgusting that someone could be so uncaring to another human. Mum had to build up confidence to ask for help when she couldn't even see who was there and that's frightening. If she wasn't so resilient, she might be too scared to ask next time. When people are in need we have a duty to help them. Surely that's what makes us human?

Another time I dropped Mum home in the car. Normally I get out, run around and open the door for her but this time she opened the door before I had a chance. She was on the pavement side of the road and didn't realise someone was walking alongside her.

She opened the car door and trapped a businessman with his briefcase between the wall and the door. He couldn't move and she kept whacking him with the door, saying, "Why won't it open?"

Because he could see my mum was blind he didn't want to be rude. He was just really polite and kept his mouth shut and pretended he wasn't there and it wasn't happening. It must have hurt so much!

Mum kept whacking him with the door, shouting, "Jess, it won't open!"

I couldn't, through my laughter, tell Mum to stop for a good twenty seconds, which must have felt like a lifetime for the poor fella. Eventually, through tears of laughter, I managed to get Mum to stop whacking him and she was so apologetic, but the man, once freed from the door, took off pretty fast.

People often don't know what to do when faced with someone with a disability. They get scared when things aren't what they expect. This happens all the time and it always makes us laugh. When me and Mum start laughing we really can't stop! We're lucky we can find the humour in things.

Mum had a really big scare with her guide dog Kasey not too long ago. Mum was calling Kasey in from the garden but she wouldn't come in; luckily my stepdad, Jim, had just got back from work and went to check on her. She was at the bottom of the garden, unable to walk or to lift herself up. Kasey's faeces were jet black and she was vomiting.

Jim grabbed Kasey and put her in the back of his taxi and him and Mum both sped to the vet. She had to have a blood transfusion; we didn't know if she'd make it through the night. It was terrifying. She was transferred to a specialist veterinary surgery because she wasn't getting better and losing weight rapidly, whilst being unable to eat. It took about two weeks under the care of the specialist vets but thankfully she pulled through.

However, she wasn't well enough to keep working as a guide dog as the illness had really taken its toll on her body, so they had to retire her from guide dog duty early. She can't work anymore. We think she ate something poisonous, maybe out in the street. It was touch and go whether she'd survive or not.

I was so scared about what would happen if she died. It held Mum back a bit at the time and dented her confidence, because whilst Kasey was sick Mum was on the waiting list at The Guide Dogs for the Blind Association to receive her new dog. It meant she had a long while of being alone and unable to get out the house while she waited.

Even though Kasey had been retired, Mum was allowed to keep her as a pet. This doesn't happen in all circumstances, but because Mum has my stepdad to help and they have a nice size garden the charity deemed it safe for both human and dog to let her stay. We were overjoyed. Kacey is still a huge part of our family. We're so happy that Kasey is okay and by the looks of it—and the way she now lies on the sofa with Mum—she's very much enjoying retirement.

I've always been a dog person, but I had no idea how much a guide dog can change your life. They are the most incredible creatures in the world. It was about seven years ago when Kasey joined our family. If Mum goes to leave the room, Kasey watches her to see if she needs help and will often get up and follow her out. They have a really special connection.

I've owned dogs in the past and I've always felt like Kasey looks at them disdainfully, like they're these peasant dogs because she's so much better trained than mine were!

Mum tries her best to keep on top of things. Mentally, she has bad days about being blind and sometimes she gets extremely frustrated with herself and members of the family if she thinks we're being careless, but we have to work together to make it as easy for her as possible.

It's not like when she first went blind though; now she knows what she needs to do to keep track of things regarding how she can help herself and lift her spirits. Don't get me wrong, there are often tough days, but now Mum makes sure she gets in touch with different charities like the Ski for Light charity. They take her cross-country skiing with special guides. She loves it because it's so freeing for her to feel the wind against her face. She can pick up some speed, which at home could mean bumping into something and hurting herself. She goes twice a year and thoroughly looks forward to the trips.

I take Mum to a running club in Haslemere on Tuesdays and Thursdays and I'm her guide. It's so good for her mental and physical health.

Mum's taught me just to laugh at things that we can't control, for example, one time she had a doctor's appointment, so we got dressed and headed out. I've got a pair of brown Timberland boots and she's got a pink pair, and it was only in the surgery that I realised she had accidently put on her pink boot on her left foot and my brown one on her right.

I said, "Mum, there's something I've got to tell you, please don't be upset!"

When I explained she found it so funny. She doesn't get upset by these things. We had to pretend that was her new look.

Another time we were in the gym. She was on the treadmill with her earphones in and she was really getting into it, dancing to her music. There were these girls taking the piss, laughing at her because she looked so funny, dancing along with a big smile on her face, but I couldn't shout at them because then Mum would realise someone had been making fun of her.

I got on a treadmill, put my earphones in and copied her, dancing, so that there were two of us, and now Mum wasn't on her own. It was the best way to deal with it. I wanted the girls to feel like idiots for being judgemental. Who was happier—those girls for being judgemental or my mum, dancing and listening to music without a care in the world? Sometimes in life what people think of you is really not worth your attention.

CHAPTER TWO

Domestic Violence

I found this chapter the hardest to write because it affects family members and reflects a great deal of pain, but I don't feel my story would make much sense without touching on it. It's a huge part of my childhood and it's the reason for many of my life choices and how I became the person I am now.

I will give you a few examples of things I saw and how they affected me. Out of respect for my family and younger generations in my family, I would like to keep the people involved anonymous.

At the age of twenty-seven or twenty-eight, I was seeing a counsellor who diagnosed me with post-traumatic stress disorder (PTSD). It all made sense. I had started on a road of self-love and was trying to understand my depression and anxiety. I wanted to fix thought patterns that served me only in a negative way.

I had to do some intense soul-searching, and it was no surprise that I had some mental health issues. I had witnessed horrific things at a young age in my home: domestic abuse between my mother and a family member.

From about the age of ten I witnessed physical fights within my family. I struggled to focus at school because I wouldn't sleep well at night. I would wait for every family member to fall asleep before I felt safe to do so. It went on for about two or three years, so my nervous system was always on red alert. I didn't know how to settle my brain and I was always in fight-or-flight mode from what I was witnessing in the home, which would then extend into every part of my life; from my relationships to my work life. Now I see how I have brought this into my adult life.

The first time I ever witnessed violence in the home was horrific. My mother and the family member started shouting at each other (alcohol-fuelled, as it was most of the time). It started with them saying really foul things to each other then it escalated to a physical fight. I was petrified. I remember a knock at the front door. I'd never been so happy to hear it. It was about nine o'clock at night and I ran down, opened the door and saw a friend of the family; he was a huge, tall guy and he ran up the stairs to break it up.

But that wasn't the end. I think once the barrier of respect had been broken, everything just deteriorated. The fights would happen more and more, but there wasn't always someone there to save us. I would be on the phone to 999 regularly asking the police to come and break it up.

Another time that was particularly terrifying was when I had come back from holiday with my mum and her boyfriend at the time. I must have been about eleven years old. It was late at night. A fight broke out and the family member attacked Mum and her boyfriend. It got so bad that I told them we had to leave the flat and we hid behind a bin down an alleyway. I saw the family member coming up the road looking for us. I made Mum stay silent. I was in my little pyjamas, barefoot, out in the street hiding my main caregivers. I was too scared to be cold.

The police car drove up towards our flat and that was when I knew I was safe. I jumped out from behind the bins where I was hiding my mum and her boyfriend, and I ran to the police car. The police got out and began to ask questions and the family member was taken away in the car, whilst another police officer took the rest of us back to the flat to talk to us, write statements and see if we were okay. By this time the sun had started to rise.

I'll give one more example of the violence—if I gave you them all this chapter would go on forever and it would be hard to relive it all over again.

I was sitting at home alone; it was a school night. Mum and her boyfriend at the time were in the pub and the other family member was out too. I was watching *The Darling Buds of May* (the TV series with David Jason; my favourite male actor of all time). I remember watching TV and just sobbing. I couldn't understand why my life wasn't like this show, where there was so much love and security. I also had bad butterflies in my tummy because I knew that with Mum being out drinking with her boyfriend and with the other family member there too, all hell could break loose at any moment. I was right.

Almost on cue the front door to the flat burst open; the family member had bloodshot eyes and was shouting, "Where are they?"

The family member had a big metal pole. I was praying that Mum and her boyfriend didn't come back any time soon and that I would be able to try to defuse the situation, but I couldn't. With shit-luck timing, Mum and her boyfriend returned home right at that minute. It quickly escalated. Mum's boyfriend was being beaten to a pulp down the side of Mum's bed and I was clawing at the family member to try to get them off, but it was no use. As a tiny eleven-year-old my input was useless. I was flung to the other side of the room like a ragdoll.

Mum got punched to the face and that's when I ran to the phone to call the police. I heard a huge bang like someone had fell to the floor.

"I think my mum's dead," I said to the operator.

They eventually sent their units of police cars, which was a regular occurrence.

This particular boyfriend of my mum's was also hard work. There's never an excuse for the violence I witnessed, but it stemmed from a lot of jealousy between Mum, her boyfriend and the family member.

When I was eleven, I went on a mini-break to a caravan park with this boyfriend, his elderly mother and my mum. I was helping Mum back from the bar because at this point she was still registered partially sighted and couldn't see well in the dark. I was used to helping her when it was too dark for her to walk back safely. So I was guiding her while her boyfriend was walking with his mum.

I could hear him raising his voice whilst Mum and I were only a few steps in front, and he started shouting that I was a "jealous little bitch" trying to take Mum away from him. He carried on shouting stuff like that until we reached our caravan. I was holding in my tears because I wasn't doing anything of the sort; I was just trying to help my mum.

Inside, the caravan the walls were thin and I could hear him still kicking off about me. It wasn't a nice feeling. It made me feel like a spare part, an inconvenience, rather than a loved child.

In our rented family home I saw bloodstains all over my bedroom floor from where the family member had slit their wrists. When I was ten, they put a tie around their neck to hang themselves with and I had to cut them down. So like I said, I saw a lot at a very young age and I'm so damn proud of how I have used that to become a better person now that I'm in my thirties.

Don't get me wrong, having to go through that was just hell and being unable to understand my emotions towards things whilst I was growing up was really hard. That led to poor relationship and life choices, especially in my early adult life. But I guess without that I wouldn't be who I am now. There is a silver lining in everything. We just have to find it.

CHAPTER THREE

Lost in the Woods

When I was about twelve years old I started to get anxious all the time. I just wanted to sit in a ball on my own in the corner of my bedroom. I had vivid nightmares of the domestic abuse I witnessed in my house, and if I ever heard anyone raise their voice I'd instantly start shaking.

I liked to sit in my room and write stories and scripts or do drawings. My pictures were always strange. I was in my room once, drawing knives, eyes, skulls; all sorts of scary things. I think I was drawing images I'd seen in my nightmares.

This made me hate school. I was so tired because I was staying awake way past midnight. I didn't like being apart from my mum. I was always a bit of a mummy's girl. I started worrying about her all the time. I'd pretend I was ill so I could stay at home with her. Eventually the school told me off for not coming in enough. I didn't really hate school, but I hated the idea of it. When I was there I usually had a good day.

I was a lot smaller than the other girls my age. My best friend Alex was a week older than me but well over a head taller. It never really bothered me, but Mum took me to the doctor's and I was transferred to a paediatrician. After lots of tests they found out my back wasn't growing in the way it should, which was why I was so little. Their main concern was that if I hit puberty before my back grew properly I would stay that small forever. I had to start taking oestrogen tablets once a day for two years.

The only time my size started to bother me was when the boys at school would tease me, especially when the other girls hit puberty and started growing boobs. I had no boobs at all and the boys would always say things like, "Jess is too small to need a bra!"

Whilst taking the oestrogen tablets, I got my first pube at about fourteen years old. I was over the moon!

Finally, I thought to myself, *I'm becoming a woman.*

I checked on it daily; I didn't want it to go anywhere, especially seeing that no others had sprouted along to join the lone ranger. I kept twiddling it to make sure it was still there, until one day I twiddled it too much and it was accidentally plucked from its place. Unfortunately, puberty was not yet meant to be.

In Year Nine, I started to hang out with a few of the naughty kids at school at lunch and break times. Some of the older kids knew my big brother Joe—we were nearly seven years apart in age—but even though we had different dads it didn't feel like we were anything other than full brother and sister. Neither of our dads lived with us, and we would fight without fail every day!

So at school, Joe's friends who were in the final years of school would talk to me and I thought that was cool, so I started hanging out with them. I never really did anything bad, but I would stand with them when they were smoking, thinking I was grown.

I made friends with two girls who were sisters; one in my year, and the other in the year above. I'd hang out at their house sometimes. One time I was round at their house, and their dad and stepmum went out for the day and left us to our own devices. We were messing about when one of the sisters suggested we should go to their neighbour's house. He had a computer and we could play on it. They'd been there before to play a few times. We didn't have any way of playing computer games where we were, so off we went.

I thought he was odd. He was tall, large build, about fifty or sixty, with no apparent wife, partner or family. He was friendly to us. We went upstairs to his computer in his bedroom. He offered us a drink and then went downstairs, saying we could play for as long as we wanted. We started playing games on his PC, and we found this programme on his computer where you could draw pictures by moving a cursor around the screen, so we spent ages doing that. We wanted to print off some of the pictures we'd made but the printer didn't have any paper, so I opened some cupboards to try to find some. I opened one drawer and stared in horror at what I saw.

On the pages in front of me were young boys being sexually abused by grown men. Some of the boys were very young—three or four years old.

I showed the girls and said, "We need to get out of here." I hid some of the pictures up my top and suggested a get-out plan. "We need to pretend your dad will be home soon. Let's say we have left chips in the oven and he will be cross if we burn them and will probably come round to get us!"

We ran downstairs and told him our story. He was quite upset we were leaving so soon. He said we should wait a bit longer as he had a friend coming over who would love to meet us. At that point I realised we were in a dangerous situation.

I sprang into action and said, "We'll come straight back, we promise. We just want to go back together."

With that he let us out of the house and we ran like hell back to the girls' house.

I phoned my mum, who was in the pub, and she sent a taxi to pick me up, and the two sisters stayed locked up in their house. My mum rang the police and I had to go down to the station to make a statement. As I was so young I had to be put in a room with the police officer and it was streamed on video to my mum in the next room so she could see and hear everything that was going on in the interview.

Mum was crying but I felt like a hero. I wasn't a victim. I was lucky that this creature had never laid a hand on me. I felt that by finding these pictures I had somehow, somewhere, saved another boy or girl in the future. I was proud of myself.

Mum regularly tried to talk to me about the incident as I think she was worried about my mental state, having to see those images at such a young age.

Once, Mum and I were walking through town and the man was heading straight towards me. I froze on the spot and started shaking uncontrollably. I started crying and told Mum it was him. She held me close and we walked quickly. Once he'd passed I was a nervous wreck. It took me a good few minutes standing still with Mum cuddling me before I could get my breath back.

Many years later, Mum told me that he had his computer seized by the police, and he left the area. I have no idea if he went to jail.

When I was young, I lived at Nan and Grandad's house in Motspur Park in south-west London with my mum and my brother. My mum and dad broke up a little while after I was born. I have no recollection of them being together. After being with Nan and Grandad, we moved to Grayswood in Surrey.

Grayswood was an amazing place for us to grow up. There were acres of woodland just screaming out for us to explore and we were always out adventure-hunting. I used to hang out with my best friend Alex.

Alex has been such a firm friend in my life up to this day. I'd say we're more like sisters than just friends. We know each other so well. I see her as the protective older sister I always wished I had. Even at school, if someone picked on me, Alex would be there to rescue me. She put one of the bigger boys who was picking on me into a skip! She literally picked him up and dropped him in. People soon knew not to mess with me because they'd have Alex on their case.

In our mid-twenties, we rented a flat together. It was so much fun living in the same place as her. Alex knows me so well; she could tell by the way I got out of bed in the mornings if I was in a bad mood.

She would hear my footsteps and yell, "What's wrong, Jess? Come in my room and tell me!"

She always gets it right. She knows my moods better than I do. I tell her my troubles and by the end she has me laughing again. I couldn't ask for a better best friend.

One day, Alex and our friend Mark—who lived down the road—and I went for an expedition into the woods. The three of us kept daring each other to keep going further and further in.

I found this awesome hill made of sand and an old frying pan lying randomly close by. We took turns sitting on the frying pan and shooting down the hill. It was so much fun. We slid down the hill over and over, for hours and hours. We messed around in the trees, playing games, forgetting about anything else in the world, running around, until we realised we were totally and utterly lost.

We spent hours trying to find our way out and by then it had started to get dark and we knew that when we did eventually get back home we would be in so much trouble. We started shouting for help. Very quickly we were really scared.

All of a sudden a dog came running into the woods. It was a brown and white spaniel. It barked at us as if we should follow, so we did. We walked for about an hour, following the dog, and he led us to the woodland entrance. We couldn't believe it. The dog then turned around and ran off again. Saved from the woods by a magic dog! I suppose magic dogs have become a regular in my life now; just look at how magic the guide dogs are.

Another time we had gone into a different part of the woods and got lost again. This time we got so lost our parents had sent out a search party to look for us. Eventually we were found by Alex's dad. He spotted us whilst driving along a road three towns away from where we'd started. Our parents were so mad at us, but we'd just been exploring. Now that I'm older I realise how scared they must have been. Oops!

Alex had a nice three-bedroom house in Grayswood, with a small playroom on the middle floor. The playroom had a window in the centre and Alex used to stand on the window ledge and jump out onto the grass below. It was pretty high up.

One day I thought I'd be brave and give it a go too, although I was totally petrified. I sat on the window ledge after Alex had already pushed herself off. I looked down nervously. Alex was shouting up, "Just push yourself off and avoid the thorn bush, then you'll be fine!"

I counted to three but instead of pushing off I closed my eyes and slid off. I messed it up so badly. My t-shirt caught on the window and I was hanging by it as if I had been hung out on the washing line to dry. There was absolutely no way of getting me down other than waiting until my t-shirt ripped, and when it did I knew I was heading straight down into the thorn bush. I just hung there, holding on until I heard the inevitable rip; my t-shirt tore and I landed in the thorns and, my God, did it hurt. I was pulling thorns out of my bottom for hours.

Even though it hurt so much, I mainly felt bad about my t-shirt, and panicked that my mum was going to be so mad at me for ripping it. Alex decided we'd try to sew it up. We went through to the kitchen to find a needle and thread, but all we could find was fishing wire and a needle. Needs must, so we decided to make the repairs with the tools we had.

We did a terrible job, as you can imagine. When I got home and explained what happened to Mum she burst out laughing. This is one of her favourite stories, which she always tells people.

Whenever I think of my mum she is laughing at something; a story she's just remembered or something she's watched on TV. Her laugh is the happiest sound in the world but most definitely the loudest I've ever heard. Every time she has a hearty laugh everyone stares!

It was clearly destiny that Alex and I would become friends; there are so many similarities between us. She has an older half-sister and I have an older half-brother. Alex has witnessed things in her home life that would be frightening for children; she too had to deal with raised voices and the constant arguments. We were going through similar problems from such a young age that it was inevitable we'd have a lifelong bond.

When I turned seven, Mum had a new boyfriend called Mikey and they decided to move in together. So we moved from our little country town up to Motspur Park, to the house next door to my nan. I had to leave Alex behind, and there would be no more woodland adventures. I had to find other things to do.

My brother, Joe played the PlayStation a lot and I got some roller skates and spent the days zooming up and down the street outside our house. Joe, had roller skates too and we found a roller disco every Saturday night for kids.

Nan used to drive us to the hall every week. It was so much fun. They would have races for pairs where one of you would be standing up and the other squatting down, and you were pushed by the standing partner. I was small enough to make sure we could go super quick.

One time, the race had started and off we went. We were doing so well; everyone else had either fallen over or dropped out. There were only three pairs left in the race, and me and Joe were in the lead. We got to the last corner, still ahead of the other two pairs, when suddenly the couple in second place stuck their feet out and tripped us over! We were out of the race.

Joe and I were so angry and the cheating team didn't get disqualified. We went home devastated. The prize for winning the race was only free entry to next week's disco, but still, me and my brother were robbed. It was so unfair. The cheek of it!

No matter what I'm doing in my life, whether it's the *Big Brother* house or filming *Ex on the Beach*, it's being tripped up when we were winning the roller skating race that still haunts me the most.

CHAPTER FOUR

Italia Conti

I always loved to act an dance and there were opportunities to do both at my school, Woolmer Hill in Haslemere, but never to a standard of a real performing arts centre. I found the Italia Conti Arts Centre (which was an associate school of the main full-time school in central London) in Guildford on the old (super slow) internet. I applied to join the part-time course and was ecstatic when I was accepted.

I was nowhere near as talented as the other children who went there, but I was willing to put in the work and get my dancing and acting skills to a high standard. I was a long way behind the other girls in ballet as they had been dancing since toddler years. I learnt quickly though; my ballet teacher was impressed with how I could pick up the dance discipline. This made me work harder. I got an idea of what progress felt like and it drove me even more.

I still have this drive and determination in me, although that can be both a blessing and a curse. If I'm not working or bettering myself constantly, I can be really hard on myself and start to feel quite down.

I spent my Saturdays mastering the basics of ballet, tap and modern jazz. At thirteen years old, I came to the conclusion that once a week at theatre school was simply not going to cut it; I needed to put more hours in. I knew there was something called the Pro Course. This would mean I would have to get the train to Guildford three times a week: Thursdays after school, Fridays after school and all day on Saturdays, but that sounded perfect to me. The more the better! Obviously, with Mum's eye condition, she couldn't drive me to the classes, but I already knew the train and bus routes from travelling there and back on Saturdays.

For the audition I had to make up routines for tap, ballet and modern jazz, as well as a song and two acting pieces, and to my massive relief they accepted me on to the course.

After about three months, I knew I needed more. A few of the kids on my course went to the full-time Italia Conti Academy of Theatre Arts at the Barbican in London. If I was going to do this properly, I needed to do that too. That way I would be able to dance and sing every day of the week.

Hundreds of well-known actors, models and singers have been to the Italia Conti Academy of Theatre Arts. It's like a school, but with an extra focus on performing arts. Naomi Campbell, Russell Brand and Martine McCutcheon studied there as well as legendary British names such as Wendy Richard, Noël Coward and Leslie Phillips. I was desperate to be an actress. My acting heroes were Julia Roberts and David Jason. I'll still watch anything that either of them is in.

I got in touch with the school and received an application form for an audition. I was really excited about auditioning again. It's such a prestigious school and I was really proud of what I'd prepared.

On the morning of the audition, Mum and I got ready to travel into central London. I got washed and dressed in my new tracksuit, and suddenly I heard Mum screaming from her bedroom. I ran into her room to find a little blackbird flapping round. At the same moment that I ran in, she ran out, locking the door behind her. Mum had totally panicked and because the bird and I were stuck in the room together, it pooped all over me before flying out of the window to freedom!

"Mum, can you let me out now? It's gone!" I shouted.

She couldn't believe she had locked me in the room out of sheer panic! Being covered in bird poop meant I had to quickly wash and find clean clothes again. Not a great start for such an important day.

Once we finally arrived at the school, my nerves kicked in. I'm sure I'd have been fine if it hadn't been for the bird incident. I walked into reception, gave my name and was sent to the waiting room, where I sat full of nerves and worries. Sometimes you know it's just not going to be your day.

After about thirty minutes, my name was called out and I was taken down to the audition studio and met the panel; all well-respected teachers from each field in the school. Off I went with my first routine. They stopped me after thirty seconds and moved me on to the next routine, and I messed that one up too. The acting went well, but I didn't do very well with the song. None of the panel showed any kind of emotion or sympathy and I knew I wasn't getting in. I was totally heartbroken. I'd worked so hard and it had fallen apart because of that stupid bird!

A few weeks later the letter arrived, just before I set off to school for the day. I opened it but I already knew what it was going to say. My audition had been unsuccessful. I'd known it from the moment I had set foot in that waiting room. I was in pieces. I walked to school crying, and when I was there I cried so much the school had to phone Mum and say I should go home early. I was inconsolable.

I'd wanted this more than anything, but I remember having this really strong realisation that feeling sorry for myself wasn't going to achieve anything, so I shook it off. I phoned the Italia Conti Academy and said, "Please let me audition again. If I get in, I will repeat my school year."

I basically volunteered to be held back a year in school so I could get extra training. Surprisingly they agreed. The next auditions were in six months. So now I had six months to get together an amazing audition to blow their socks off and get me into the school. I was so relieved to have been given a second chance. I had to get it right this time.

I must have driven them crazy as I was constantly on the phone to the receptionist asking more and more irrelevant questions, just to make sure I was always on their mind. They must have thought, *Oh no, it's that Jess girl again!*

For the next six months I kept going to school and to the part-time course in Guildford, but I didn't want to waste any time or opportunities. I knew I needed to be as good as possible for this next audition, so instead of having my lunch break I'd always find a teacher who was having a break and make them help me with my routines. For six months I ate, slept and breathed acting and dancing. It was all I thought about; all I wanted to do. That's still the way I feel now.

Eventually the six months passed. I went back for my audition and guess what? I nailed it. I knew it was going well and the panel seemed really impressed. They said they'd let me know in the next week or so. Waiting for that letter to come through the post was the most tense week of my entire life.

It was lunchtime at school when I got the phone call from Mum. She said, "Jess, you've had a big letter come through the post from Italia Conti. I've opened it. You got in, but before you get too excited, you need to know you didn't get a scholarship, so I'm really sorry, but I'm not sure we will be able to let you go. It's expensive and I don't earn enough money to send you. I may be able to scrape together half your school fees, but unless your dad can chip in, it's just not going to be possible."

I was heartbroken. To be accepted, but then not to be able to go because it was so expensive just wasn't fair.

I phoned my dad. Even though Mum and Dad separated when I was a baby I was still very much in contact with him and would often see him at the weekends. He told me that he'd have to check his finances and let me know that evening.

I couldn't concentrate on anything for the rest of the day at school. I was just thinking of fundraising ideas to make sure I could get in if Dad wasn't able to help me. That night he called. He said he would have to remortgage the house and then him and Mum could work together and there would just about be enough money. . . but they would make it work. If I promised to work hard, they would find a way for me to go.

I couldn't believe it! I will forever and a day be thankful to my parents for pulling together on this. We accepted my place at the school, and it was time for the fun to begin.

We went out to buy my new school uniform, which was only available at Harrods in London. My amazing Nan and Grandad had offered to pay for the uniform, which was a massive help. We went on a girls' day out to Harrods. It cost well over two hundred pounds to buy everything I needed. Everyone was coming together for me. It was better than Christmas! I was living my dreams because of the hard work I'd put in and the generosity and love of the people around me who knew how much I wanted this.

After a long summer, my first day came. I was desperate to start my new school. I'd even had to move into my nan and grandad's house in order to go to Italia Conti, because it was closer to London and the train tickets were more affordable.

It wasn't what I expected though. The classes were small; I think there were twelve people in mine, and everyone was a tight-knit group. I came in hoping to make friends right away but it wasn't that easy. I had this terrible feeling of self-doubt and inadequacy. I found it hard to talk to the other kids, and when I did I went bright red and got sweaty with nerves.

On my first lunch break I walked up to the canteen, but couldn't find anywhere to sit, so I walked to the toilets and sat and ate my lunch locked in the toilet cubicle. I did this for about a week and started to wonder if I had made the wrong choice coming to this school, which was crazy because I wanted this more than anything.

When you want things so badly you can get so scared. The standard of talent around me was unbelievable and I felt way out of my depth.

Every day when I got home from school I cried. This lasted about four weeks. One day, one of the girls who I had made friends with said, "If you're not fitting in and don't like it, maybe you should think about leaving."

It was the kick up the backside I needed. The thought of leaving after all that—no bloody way! It was a real boost. My fight came back to me. I didn't know where it had disappeared to for those first few weeks. Time to work even harder, Impiazzi!

From that moment on I put everything into every class. I practised dances routines at lunch and dinner breaks. I practised in my bedroom after school. I continued going to the Guildford Saturday school, and on the way back to my mum's for the weekend, I'd stop off in Covent Garden and do an extra class in Latin jazz on Fridays. I literally didn't stop, hoping my persistence would pay off.

The teachers were noticing my progress and I started getting solos in class and being picked to lead warm-ups. My confidence started to soar again. After a scary and nervous start, I had pulled through and was showing people how talented I was.

It's a huge credit to the school that they let me be part of it. I was technically nowhere near the other girls and boys who had seven to ten years of dance experience, but they believed in me and I believed in myself, and I got there. Having the teachers and principal believing in you as a child also really helps. Anne Sheward, the Italia Conti principal, always really encouraged me and it made me want to work harder.

I was made a prefect when I hit my final school year. I was so happy and proud, and quite frankly more than a little surprised. I was a good kid. I worked hard at the things I liked. I didn't enjoy the academic classes that were at the first part of each day. After lunch, it was our vocational training (dancing, acting, singing). For four or five days a week I'd be late to school so that I could miss Maths. I've never been great with numbers, something that still rings true in my adult life, but thankfully, so far I haven't had to worry about algebra or square roots (fingers crossed for me). I was also terrified of my Maths teacher, so that didn't help matters.

I had the best years of my life at Italia Conti. I was constantly surrounded by crazy, eccentric characters. Once we had a substitute Science teacher. I felt terribly sorry for her. The poor woman had to kick some kids out the class for bad behaviour and by the end of the lesson there was only one kid left in the class! The headteacher walked past shaking his head and shouted at us to go back inside.

I think theatre kids are a different breed to other school kids and it must be a bit of a shock if you're not prepared for so many show-offs. I loved it though. I was learning so much about the industry I wanted to spend my life in. I felt like the luckiest girl in the world.

CHAPTER FIVE

Charlie

I remember the day of the London Underground bombings on July 7th 2005. That morning I was late for school (Maths was first) so I slept in late to miss the class. I put in my iPod walked to my station, jumped on the train to Waterloo and caught the number four bus to the Barbican.

I started to sense something was going on. Sitting on the top deck of my bus, looking out the window, I could see police cars and ambulances speeding around. I was used to seeing that in London but it did seem more than usual.

When I got off the bus, three teachers were stood on the front steps, looking for the Italia Conti students, pulling them inside the building and sending them up to the canteen, where the whole place was in lockdown.

I had no idea what was going on but immediately I was scared. Once inside, I looked out the window down to the busy street below and saw a few kids from our school running in, crying, covered in grey dust. No one was laughing or joking like usual. Eventually, news arrived. Four bombs had gone off; three on the London Underground, one on a London bus. The city was under attack. How many more bombings were there going to be?

The TV was on in the canteen, and we fell silent as we watched breaking news footage of what was happening on the streets around us. I remember the image of the blown-up London bus, identical to the one I had just been on, contentedly listening to music on my iPod. We sat completely still, shocked, not knowing what to do. So many people had been killed and injured around our precious city. How could this be happening?

I couldn't phone anyone as there was no phone signal. Something as normal as making a phone call was impossible with the whole of London in chaos. I wanted to get hold of my grandad because he was a London cab driver and I was so worried about him. I wanted to make sure he was safe. I kept ringing until eventually I got through. He was at the airport in a fluster, equally terrified about what was going on.

That night I couldn't get home from school. The teachers didn't want us leaving unless our parents could drive in and collect us. My mum can't drive and I didn't want my grandad coming into London just to collect me, so I chose to stay at school overnight rather than risk him making the journey.

The YMCA across the road kindly let a lot of us stay over in their spare rooms. It was one of the saddest nights of my life as I thought about everything that had happened throughout the day, and the people who had been badly affected, just because they'd come into London for the day, just as I had done that morning. The next day my grandparents drove in to collect me and took me home. I was so happy to see them. It felt like a horrible dream. I'd never seen London look so much like a ghost town.

Some of my happiest memories are from the Italia Conti end-of-year shows at the prestigious Wimbledon Theatre. The buzz of show season was like no other feeling. This was what acting was all about. This was what I'd wanted when I was practising so hard during my lunchtimes at school. I was surrounded by theatre, anticipation and excitement.

It was a chance to show off our talent, and agents were invited to watch. If you performed well anything could happen. The talent was simply amazing. Pixie Lott was in the year below me and it was clear she was going to be a big star. I've been really happy to see her do so well.

I'd watch the older girls in awe and get excited for them, knowing so many of them would go on to do amazing things, like working in the West End and in TV and film. I knew one day I'd follow in those footsteps.

I was coming to the end of my school year's course. I was so desperate to continue on to the full college course at Italia Conti. I desperately needed a scholarship or there was no way I could afford to go. I re-auditioned, putting my heart and soul into every audition piece.

My life changed forever on the May 18th 2006. I had been sent a letter from Italia Conti offering me a full scholarship to graduate from the school into the college. I was ecstatic. I couldn't stop reading the letter over and over. Being at Italia Conti had been the most important thing in my world, and not only could I stay there, but I'd got a scholarship. I was desperate to be an actress and now it felt possible; my dreams were coming true. I couldn't believe, out of all the people who had applied, I was one of the people who had been accepted.

That same day, my brother and his girlfriend Laureen were moving in together in Haslemere. Their first child, Charlie, was thirteen months old and I was helping look after him whilst they moved house. Laureen had told me Charlie was poorly so I just sat with him on the bed. He was quite tired and making a soft groaning sound. I was trying to cheer him up, but he wasn't as responsive as usual. I loved playing with Charlie. He was such an adorable little baby and I loved being Aunty Jess.

Laureen had a doctor's appointment for him at midday so when she came back to the flat the three of us went to the doctor's surgery. We weren't worried. They'd probably give him some medicine or tell us everything was fine.

We'd been at the doctor's surgery for forty-five minutes and hadn't been seen, but finally we were called to see the doctor. As soon as he was in the room Charlie's eyes rolled into the back of his head and he went limp. The doctor acted immediately, and put an oxygen mask on him and called an ambulance. I didn't panic, because there were doctors around, and they were taking charge, but Laureen burst into tears. I remember her screaming, "My baby, my baby!"

I let out a nervous little laugh and said, "Don't be silly, he'll be fine!"

Little did I realise how wrong I was. Laureen jumped into the ambulance with Charlie and the paramedic. I stayed at the doctor's surgery and phoned my brother to tell him what was happening. Within five minutes he sped round, picked me up and we went full-speed to the hospital. On the way, I spotted a lone magpie on the road in front of our car. I have always been superstitious and remembered the magpie rhyme 'One for Sorrow, Two for Joy.' My stomach turned and I realised something really bad was happening.

Charlie was rushed straight into intensive care as soon as he got to the Royal Surrey Hospital in Guildford. They were running all sorts of tests. My brother Joe, Laureen and myself were put in the family room whilst they tried to save his life. Eventually, they diagnosed him with Meningococcal meningitis. He deteriorated rapidly and unfortunately we lost little Charlie.

It was a hard thing to get my head around. Joe and Laureen literally just walked out of the hospital dumbfounded. I found a quiet place around the side. I threw my bag on the floor and punched a wooden fence as hard as possible to stop me from screaming out loud.

I rang my mum and Jim, who were on holiday in Turkey, and Mum screamed down the phone. I then rang my best friend Alex, who was in Tesco's, and she broke down in tears. I took a deep breath and in a daze made my way back into the hospital.

We went into the ward, where they put Charlie's body in a Moses basket. The nurses pulled the curtains around us so we could spend some last moments with him. I put my finger in his hand as if he were holding it.

Eventually Uncle David, Aunty Susan and Nan and Grandad came to pick me up to take me to Nan and Grandad's house in Motspur Park. Uncle David walked in first and completely broke down. It must have been a horrid shock to open the curtain in a rush and see our Charlie's lifeless body.

I don't really remember leaving the hospital. I guess my brain managed to block some things out.

Mum got home the following morning after trying her best to return from Turkey in the quickest time possible, and we organised visiting Charlie in the Chapel of Rest in the hospital. My nan, Uncle David and Aunty Susan came with us. I didn't want to go in with the family; I wanted to see him on my own. I found it hard being around the adults grieving because I wanted to help them.

After saying goodbye and giving a kiss to Charlie, I went back up the stairs to the main hospital where my family were waiting for me. Suddenly an overwhelming feeling of dark sadness flushed through my body. I ran to the staircase. I didn't want to be around anyone. I found a corner a few flights down and cried; the kind of cry that takes your entire breath away.

Then I started to panic. I couldn't breathe and everything started to spin. A doctor passing by saw me and got a paper bag for me to breathe into, and after calming me down, took me back to my family. I was trying to be strong for them, but I couldn't any more. This was too much.

Charlie's funeral was a beautiful service; at least as beautiful as a funeral can be. I wore white jeans and a blue shirt. We didn't want everyone wearing black. Charlie was a baby and babies like colours. Wearing black felt inappropriate. My stepdad Jim wore a Tigger tie because Charlie loved Winnie-the-Pooh. Jim was known for his crazy ties.

I remember being upset for forgetting to put my teddy bear necklace on. It was such a pointless thing for me to get worked up about, but I think getting upset about things that were irrelevant stopped me from dealing with the things that actually hurt. I didn't understand how Charlie could have died. How would my brother and Laureen deal with that? One day you have a baby and the next day you don't.

When we got to the church it was quiet. Nobody knew what to say. I walked to the front and took my seat next to Shonagh, Laureen's sister I was shaking uncontrollably. I had a role in the service. I'd been asked to read a poem called 'Little Angels.'

Charlie's tiny coffin was carried down the aisle. His Tigger toy was at the altar with a beautiful photograph taken on his first birthday just a month before.

The vicar had told me that if I couldn't get to the end of the poem it wasn't a problem; she would finish it for me. When it was my turn, I stood at the front of the church and read the poem out.

"When God calls little children
to dwell with Him above,
we mortals sometimes question
the wisdom of His love. . ."

I could feel a lump in the back of my throat. I looked over at my family. They were crying. I couldn't cope. I took a deep breath and tried to continue.

"For no heartache compares
with the death of one small child,
who does so much to make our world
seem wonderful and mild.
Perhaps God tires of calling
the aged to His fold
so He picks a rosebud
before it can grow old."

I cracked and started sobbing. I couldn't help it.

I looked up; people were looking at me. Others had their heads down. It was too much. I could sense the vicar walking towards me to help me but I didn't want her finishing *my* poem. She was a stranger and this poem was for Charlie from me, his Aunty, and I was finishing it for him, no matter what. If I cried, I cried. It was important to get through it.

I looked away from the vicar, took a deep breath, closed my eyes and continued.

"God knows how much we need them
and so He takes but few,
to make the land of heaven
more beautiful to view.
Believing this is difficult
still somehow we must try,
the saddest word mankind knows
will always be goodbye.
So when a child departs
we who are left behind
must realise God loves children,
angels are hard to find."

I folded my poem and went back to my seat. I had got to the end. I did it for Charlie.

Laureen took to the altar to read out her poem. She was so brave, but I think she was still in complete shock. She read without tears and quickly returned to her seat. She looked totally numb and it broke everyone's heart.

We left the church to Charlie's favourite song:

Down in the jungle where nobody goes
there's a great big gorilla washing his clothes.
With a rub-a-dub here and a-rub-a-dub there
that's the way he washes his clothes.
Diddle-I-dee, a boogie woogie
Diddle-I-dee, a boogie woogie
that's the way he washes his clothes.

It took a long time to register what I'd read that morning in the letter; I was graduating to the Italia Conti College. It seemed impossible that it was something I could possibly be excited about. A few days ago it had been the only important thing in my life, but now it didn't feel like anything, really. It felt like there was no point in anything at all.

In the end I left Italia Conti when my mum lost her eyesight. It meant I didn't get my BA Honours. Even though I left in such horrible circumstances, having the opportunity to go to such an incredible school was one of the best things that ever happened to me.

CHAPTER SIX

My Mum

In my book, I didn't just want to write about how Mum got through losing her sight and how amazing she is for pulling through. I wanted to write a chapter that helps people understand the dark times that people with disabilities have. There have been so many times in interviews when I have praised my mum and what she has managed to do, but I feel leaving out the dark times gives everyone half a story.

I also wanted to make sure anyone reading this with sight issues knows that the dark times are normal. I want to help people in similar situations and raise awareness for those who don't understand what it's like to live with sight loss. So I thought, what better way than sharing my mum's own words? So yes, this chapter is dedicated to her, but interview-style, so her voice can be heard, warts and all!

ME: Mother dearest, aka Lady Deborah of Haslemere, Surrey, thank you for giving up some time to help with this chapter of my book, which is all about you! I'd like to start at the beginning, when you realised that your sight was going to go and when the reality of it first hit you. Talk us through the emotions.

DEBBIE (my mum): The first time I realised I was going to lose my sight, I was on my honeymoon. I was walking down some steps and I realised they had started to blend together.

I came back from holiday and booked a private appointment at Moorfields Eye Hospital, as I needed to know what was going on. I saw my usual doctor. He looked into my eyes, sat back in his chair, took a deep breath and said, "We thought this might happen. You're starting to lose your sight. If we operate, we could open a can of worms that may make it worse."

At this point it was only my right eye that was a problem. I knew I could cope with sight in one eye. I was with my husband and once we left the hospital I was dumbfounded. I just felt numb. I knew I'd still have the use of my other eye, however, in the back of my mind, I knew I had the same condition in both eyes. If this had happened to one of them, chances were it would happen to both, but I didn't want to think about that. I needed to focus on the positives.

ME: When you realised the second eye was going, how did you cope?

DEBBIE: I was still working when my left eye started to deteriorate, and I knew it was going fast when I'd judge how much of the screen I could see on my work computer. I've always been long-sighted, so I just thought I'd have to get thicker glasses. The reality of it hit after every weekend passed, and I went back to work, it became apparent I wouldn't be able to see even with the thicker glasses. That wouldn't have helped at all, because the problem wasn't things becoming blurry, it was more like a thick, grey fog closing around my eyes that I couldn't see through.

On September 16th 2007, I ran the London 10K with you, Jess. I completed it independently and that was the last thing I did by myself, before realising I could no longer do things alone. When I realised that my sight was failing rapidly, I was at work at my computer. My husband Jim picked me up for lunch and I broke down in tears and didn't stop crying for about three hours. It finally hit me that I couldn't see any more, no matter how much I tried to pretend it wasn't happening. It was also the last time I went into work. That was on February 29th 2008.

ME: I remember this time. I was still at Italia Conti and I've spoken about this earlier in the book. When you were unable to work you were terrified.

I came home and you hadn't left the sofa where I'd left you earlier that day. That story was from my point of view, but I want to know what went through your mind that day? You must have felt so scared.

DEBBIE: In the early stages I'd wake up in the morning and I'd simply lie there in bed because today would be no different from yesterday, and it'd probably be the same tomorrow. I felt a big cloud come over me, like a depression. Every day I remember taking a deep breath and getting out of bed just to use the bathroom, and I would think, *Bloody hell, here we go again*.

There was no joy in each day. I felt like my life had come to a sudden halt. I had a visit from SAVI, which is a charity now called Sight for Surrey, and they gave me some devices to help me get through daily tasks. They also arranged to send me audiobooks and audio newspapers through the Royal National Institute for the Blind (RNIB). These were great, however I soon realised all I was doing was listening to other people's problems and sadness in the news and magazines.

I felt like I was spiralling. I never felt suicidal, but I do remember having a thought that if I didn't wake up the next day, it didn't matter to me, that would be just fine. Trying to explain to family and friends about how I was feeling was really frustrating because I knew they'd never fully understand. That brought with it resentment and anger. I was short-tempered and there were plenty of tears.

ME: So there was clearly a point in your life when you knew this way of living wasn't going to serve you? Talk me through how you changed it.

DEBBIE: After staying in bed for six months and achieving nothing, and still feeling the same horrible depression, I realised something had to change. I happened to be listening to a book by Frank Gardner called *Blood and Sand*, which is about his last visit to Riyadh in Saudi Arabia. As it happened, I'd lived there back in 1980 for a few years and I was instantly drawn to the book for that reason. The book is a memoir on how he was shot and his cameraman murdered by terrorists. Frank lost the use of his legs after the horrific ordeal. After that, Frank Gardner still worked for the BBC. He didn't let his new disability stop him and that's when I knew I had to stop feeling sorry for myself and make good use of the rest of my life.

ME: What did you do differently from that moment on?

DEBBIE: Let me tell you, it wasn't an easy process. I knew I had to make changes; there was no other way. I found the telephone number for Guide Dogs and I started my application to get one. Before you get a guide dog, you need to learn routes around your area that you can map in your head. A mobility instructor from Guide Dogs started training me to use my white cane to assist me in learning and mapping out those routes. It was strange because six months before I lost my sight, I could easily walk up the street and do all this by myself and now I needed a cane and a mobility instructor to do this simple task. The first time I went out with my cane I was so scared. I felt disheartened because I really felt disabled; this was now my new life, and it was a hard pill to swallow.

My mobility instructor, Pat, and I were out one day cane training and even though I was taking lots of positive steps by this point, something just came over me and I burst out crying. Pat asked me what was wrong and I told her I just felt so disabled with this stick and I banged it on the pavement, to which she replied, "Deborah, how disabled would you feel without this stick?"

The tears instantly dried up and I thought to myself, *If Pat is spending her time coming here to help me and being so kind to me, I'm jolly well going to learn as much as I can and show her how thankful I am.*

ME: I remember when you found out about the Royal National College for the Blind (RNC) and you decided to go. It was down in Hereford. I felt nervous because I'd become very protective of you but I was happy at the same time, because I knew it would do you the world of good. It would basically retrain you to live life and learn new skills as a blind person. It was a boarding college so I knew you'd be away and I hated the thought of that, but we spoke all the time. What were your feelings about heading off to the college?

DEBBIE: The day I left for college, Jim took me down with my stuff. It was on January 4th 2010. It was a two-and-a-half-hour journey. Once we arrived, we were shown around the halls where I was going to be staying. My room was up on the third floor. We were shown the kitchen area and the fire escapes and then Jim helped me settle into my new room. When Jim had to leave for his long drive back, we gave each other a hug and we were both in floods of tears. It was the first and only time I ever said, "Why has this happened to me?"

Once Jim left, all I wanted to do was speak to my mum and dad, but I didn't call them. I knew I'd cry and with them both being elderly I really didn't want to upset them. Instead I went and had a bath and put on the song *Stronger* by Will Young. I listened to this song over and over again; it gave me a sense of courage and I knew I needed to be strong. After that I sat on my bed, drank an entire bottle of Moët Champagne, which I bought with me from home and went to sleep knowing tomorrow was a new day. A time for me to push forward with my new life.

The RNC was the best thing that happened to me. I was there for a year. I passed my exams, which included English, Maths and Holistic Therapy, and I won various awards. I became an ambassador for the college, which meant I would get to do presentations to up to fifty people in the audience. Usually the audience were job centre administrators so they'd learn how to best help employ blind and partially sighted people from our college.

I was also nominated to represent the college in Poland for Mission Clean Earth with nine other countries from Europe. I felt a great sense of achievement. I was getting on with my life and it felt amazing. I was achieving so much more than I ever realised was possible. I was even invited to join the Royal party for lunch, which included the Duke of Kent, who were visiting the college. I started at the college feeling so low, with shattered confidence. When I eventually left I was back to me again. My confidence had completely returned. It takes time to regain confidence once you lose your sight and you have to learn from mistakes and experiences.

ME: Now, let's skip forward to when you first got your phone call from Guide Dogs with the wonderful news that you'd been matched. This meant you were about to go into training with your first-ever guide dog. How did you feel?

DEBBIE: I was overjoyed when I got the phone call. I was so excited to start training with my dog. Kasey came to me on September 10th 2012. I trained from home with her, however the illusion was shattered when I realised how scary it is at first, and how much work you have to put in with your guide dog to enable you to go out with them for the first time.

I had my eight weeks of training with her before I qualified to take her out by myself on the routes that we'd learned together with my guide dog instructor. I can honestly say it was terrifying at the start; to put my life in the paws of a dog. Once again I had to build up confidence, not just in me but in my dog too. Once I conquered my fear, and Kasey and I had a great relationship built up, I felt so free. I could walk through the town and go to the shops with my head held high. Free and independent.

ME: Your story always gives me goosebumps, Mum, and I find it incredible that you changed your mindset to serve you and pull you through an incredibly tough period of your life. Could you give any advice to people who are in your situation? Or who may have family members in your situation? How can they pull through and come out the other side?

DEBBIE: Life is a struggle for many people. Having a disability adds to the daily struggles. Yes, life is tougher when you're blind. It's almost a unique disability; not being able to see puts you at the mercy of everyone. Blind people will have their own ways of doing things that work best for them, and they want to do them. Sometimes people who can see think they know better and can do it best, but we use different senses to orientate us. For example, when crossing the road, most of the time members of the public are great and can be helpful, but occasionally they—and of course our own family members—think they know best and it can feel quite demeaning.

My advice to anyone who is going through the same situation is to never give up. It is hard work to learn different skills and do the things you've always done in a different way. It takes time, confidence and experience, but you will get there. It's important to discipline your mind to make sure you get up each day and keep going.

It takes courage to be blind and the more courage I got, the more the world opened up for me. I now go skiing and running with special groups for blind people. I've never felt so free as when I have my cross-country skis on and feel that lovely cold air on my face. There is so much help out there to ensure I'm living the life I deserve.

ME: Mum, you're a star and I hope this chapter will help many people. I love you!

CHAPTER SEVEN

My Dad

I don't know where to start when talking about my dad. It's quite a tough one. I guess I'll go back to the very beginning.

My mum and dad were not together long. In fact, the only reason they stayed together longer than my mum wanted to was simply because she fell pregnant with me by accident. I have no memory of them ever being together. I've seen a few pictures of them together when I was a baby but that's it.

When we moved away from Nan and Grandad's house, my mum and dad bought a house in a beautiful little village called Grayswood in Surrey. It didn't last long though; Mum eventually broke it off and he moved out.

My early memories of my dad start with infant school. He used to pick me up after school every other Friday and I would spend the weekend at his place, which at the time was with his dad (my Grandad Sid) in Putney.

Dad was a great swimmer. I'm sure it's thanks to him that I've always been good in the water. Mum says that at the pool he would always climb up to the top diving board and do flips into the water. I have a vague memory of watching him from the café having diving lessons at Putney Leisure Centre. He was on the top diving board doing a handstand, then flipped down into the water; the perfect dive into the pool. I loved watching him diving. It was so impressive and everyone would stop to watch and gasp.

When I got older, Dad moved to Bognor Regis, by the seaside. I started bringing a friend with me every time I went to visit him. Dad would smoke and drink a lot so I got bored. He seemed to make a bit more of an effort when I brought a friend along, and would often take us to Butlins and let us loose in the pool there with all the water slides. It was so much fun.

He always liked to have a few beers, and he'd always been a heavy smoker. Gradually I noticed he was starting to become a heavy drinker; more than the usual few beers at night. He would open a can of beer the minute we got in from our weekend activity, even if it was as early as one o'clock in the afternoon. It was the first thing he did.

I also noticed he started to get a bit mean when he'd had a drink. One time, I had a friend come to his house with me. Dad bought us both a packet of Hubba Bubba and I was trying to blow the biggest bubble possible, so obviously I shoved the whole packet in my mouth. For some reason this infuriated him.

He started yelling at me, "You think you're Jack the Lad—that's what your brother thought and that's why his friend ended up dying in the crash because they thought they were Jack the Lad too."

I was only eleven or twelve and I burst out crying. I was embarrassed because my friend was there and also it was a pretty mean thing to say. I couldn't believe he was being so horrible to me in front of my friend. My brother's friend dying had such an impact on our lives. I couldn't believe my dad was mentioning it so glibly.

After a few incidents like this, I realised it wasn't a good environment for me to be in. Every time I got to his house, it stank of smoke. I was getting older, and with everything happening at home with my mum, I wanted to be there with her. I started not wanting to go to Dad's as much. I'd often make up excuses and ended up seeing him maybe two or three times a year.

As soon as I passed my driving test, I'd pop down now and then to see Dad and spend a few hours with him. I don't think he ever knew I was glamour modelling, but I told him about my jobs at the race tracks and my promo work.

One day, I did this jokey TV show for E4 with an ex-boyfriend of mine, called *Meet the Parents*. It was a set-up show with hidden cameras, basically introducing my boyfriend at the time to my family, however the family were actors in a fake house. The show was hilarious. They had the actress who was playing my mum as a sex therapist, saying really uncomfortable things to this boyfriend, who had no idea what was going on and thought this was my real family and that they were bonkers.

It was one of the first times I'd been on TV and I told my dad to watch the show and explained to him the way it worked. The show aired, and I was watching from a hotel room near a race track where I was working the next day.

I got so many calls and texts saying how great and funny the show was. Then Dad called. I could tell he was drunk because he was really slurring his words.

"Hi Dad, did you watch it? It was so funny!"

"You're a little slag! How fucking embarrassing that they'd show your boyfriend talking to a sex therapist! You're no daughter of mine."

The rant went on for a good few minutes.

I was in complete shock. I remember shouting back, "It's disgusting that you would say things like that to me!"

But he didn't apologise. He just kept going on and on. Through broken sobs I told him I didn't want to talk to him anymore and hung up. I was heartbroken.

We didn't speak for nearly a year after that. He never called to apologise, or to check if I was okay. After about a year, I decided I would be the responsible one and do the adult thing, so I called him.

The phone just rang and rang. I tried the next day, and the next, but nothing. After a couple of weeks of him not answering I started to worry. I decided to drive down to Bognor to see what was going on. I feared that maybe he was dead. My best friend Alex said she would come down on the car journey with me because it was starting to feel like something bad could have happened and she didn't want me to have to deal with anything on my own.

Alex drove us both down to the coast and we pulled up outside Dad's house. The front lawn was overgrown like a jungle. It looked awful. His sitting room window was open, so Alex climbed up to try to peek through the curtains. My heart was racing. I had visions of his corpse slumped on his chair.

"There's no one in the living room, Jess," Alex said.

We banged on the door, but there was no reply. We went to the shop next door to see if anyone had seen him. I described him to the shop assistant, who recognised the description but said he hadn't seen him for about six weeks. Before that they'd noticed he was buying bottles of vodka daily.

I started to panic and started to blame myself. Maybe it was my fault for doing that E4 show. Maybe he was so embarrassed about what he'd seen he'd gone crazy.

Still panicking about whether he was alive or dead, we knocked on his neighbours' doors, but no one had seen him. We were running out of ideas and eventually decided we should call the police.

They advised me to call the local hospitals. Alex and I started off with Chichester Hospital and with a stroke of luck, they said they did have someone by that name. He had been in intensive care for the last six weeks. We couldn't believe we'd managed to track him down. We jumped in the car and sped round to the hospital to find out what on earth had been going on.

I really wasn't prepared for what I saw. Dad was in a hospital bed and he was totally shocked to see me. It looked like he'd aged thirty years. His hair was overgrown, nails yellow and filthy. He looked like a homeless man. I spoke to him to find out what had happened, but I couldn't get a straight answer from him. He seemed confused and disoriented and I felt like he wasn't telling me the truth.

At first he said the ambulance had picked him up, but in the next sentence he said he'd driven himself to the hospital. He seemed so dazed and not in his right mind. I went to speak to a doctor to find out what was going on.

I never fully got to the bottom of it, but speaking to one of the nurses, I was told he had internal bleeding. Still to this day I'm none the wiser about what happened for him to be taken to intensive care. How had he got there? Who had found him? What was wrong? What was going on in his life? He'd asked the doctors not to tell me.

They did say he was highly intoxicated when he was brought in and it seemed he was an alcoholic. Well, that explained why he looked as he did, I guess. I was so sad to see him like that.

I realised he needed me, so I started heading down every week to see him. He would ask for cigarettes, money and extra food so I started bringing anything he needed.

When he was let out of hospital, I took him home. The house was completely and utterly filthy. The carpet looked like it had grease all over it. The house stank of cigarettes. There was paper everywhere including final demand notices for unpaid bills. I couldn't believe my eyes.

Around this time, Denny Solomona and I had moved into our first home together up north. He was getting quite mad with me because my dad would keep calling asking for money or tobacco and I would post him money. Dad told me if I put it into his bank he wouldn't be able to draw it out because he was beyond his overdraft limit.

I was concerned that he was buying alcohol with the money so I decided to start sending him food deliveries. He would call me twice a week wanting more tobacco, more food, more coffee, which started to cause me financial strain. This couldn't carry on. Supplying someone with food and cigarettes twice a week gets expensive, especially when you're trying to build a new home with your partner.

Eventually, I decided it had got too much, so I phoned Mum and asked her what the hell I was supposed to do. I couldn't leave the man to starve and if I sent food with no tobacco he would ring me ten times a day to ask me to send it.

She said she would come down to visit him with me. We were concerned about these incessant calls and the pressure he was putting on me.

So Mum and I drove down to Bognor Regis to investigate what was going on. When we got to Dad's house it still stank of smoke, and there were empty beer cans lying around everywhere. The house was a big mess. Mould was growing from the cups and plates left on the sides of the kitchen and tables. Flies were making themselves at home in the mess. It was awful.

We could see he clearly wasn't washing himself. His personal hygiene was as bad as his house. Everything just smelt disgusting. The back garden was a jungle of weeds and there were thorns climbing up so high. It was clearly an issue for environmental health.

Mum and I wanted him to be checked out and we managed to get him to agree to an appointment at the doctor's, which was a two-minute walk away.

We went to the appointment with him and Dad agreed that the blood test results were allowed to be shared with us.

Afterwards, we took him home. All we could do was wait for the results.

A few weeks passed and we heard nothing. So, again, we drove down to his house. We went to the doctor's and asked why we hadn't had the results. The doctor explained that once we left my dad had returned and told them he didn't want Mum and I to know the results and took back his permission to let us know. I was furious. It's so hard trying to help someone who refuses to help themselves.

Every time we went to visit, we tried to clean up a little around the house before we left, but it would just be in a worse state when we got back.

We tried calling the local Social Services and doctors to get help, but we were ping-ponged back to each service each time. We were at our wits' end with it.

Mum decided we should take matters into our own hands, so we started looking at the unpaid bills and bank statements to try to find out what was going on and why he was in debt.

We found out that he'd got an inheritance from my Grandad Sid. I didn't go to his funeral because no one told me he had died. I don't even think my dad went to the funeral. From the look of the bank statement, in two months Dad had spent the whole thirty thousand pounds he'd inherited, and all of it at the little shop next door to his house. He'd spent Grandad Sid's money on cigarettes and alcohol.

We started calling the people who were chasing my dad for money, getting a hold on everything until we got to the bottom of it. Mum managed to get fines dropped from the bank because clearly they were dealing with a vulnerable person.

Mum then managed to discover that my dad had not sorted out his pension, which was why no money had been going into his account. Mum got that fixed up and sorted. She even managed to get a back payment too. Mum opened up another bank account, which my dad's pension would go into, and set up lots of direct debits so his bills and his mortgage would be paid.

Mum stopped his house from being repossessed. Honestly, she was like a miracle woman. It just goes to show how mindsets work. My mum was blind and managed to do this for someone who was more 'capable' of doing it, but Dad's mindset was switched off, and he didn't care anymore.

When the finances were sorted, we got ourselves power of attorney for Dad's finances and health. I don't know what I would have done without Mum during this time, and I certainly don't know what would have happened to Dad without our intervention.

She got Dad a bank card and I would organise his weekly food parcels to make sure he had the right things to eat and drink, and of course tobacco to smoke.

The next step was operation clean-up. We hired a cleaning company who were experienced in houses in conditions like this. They set out deep cleaning and removed old shabby furniture from his home on the lowest budget possible. Finally, the house was liveable again.

My stepdad Jim spent about nine hours hacking down the weeds in the garden. We hired cleaners to go round once a week to clean up after Dad so he wouldn't allow it to get back to how it had been before.

As we now had power of attorney, we could find out what was wrong with him. We knew there must be something medically not right. How had he allowed his life to get like this? After loads of hospital appointments and scans we eventually found out that Dad has Vascular dementia (often brought on by alcohol and tobacco abuse) and Alzheimer's. It was devastating, but things started to make sense, and at least we knew what the problem was and how to handle things properly.

I used to get so mad with my dad. I never shouted at him or anything, but inside I was so upset with him for being this person. Why would he let this happen to himself? Why did he drink so much? Having the diagnosis helped because I knew he needed help and we would be there to give it.

Dad had also developed agoraphobia; he wouldn't ever dream of leaving the house alone. I think this started when he was caught stealing from the shop next door and it frightened him. This was, in a way, a saving grace because it stopped him from drinking. He could no longer get access to alcohol. However, it put a lot more pressure on Mum and me because we would get phone calls every time he ran out of something, including sugar and coffee.

Now, though, we have a great system; we've figured out what he needs and what he goes through in a week and we can judge it just about right. He gets greedy with the tobacco—he literally just sits and smokes rolled-up cigarettes one after the other. It's pretty much his only joy in life.

We have a district nurse to attend to him every morning, and to give him his medication, because he wasn't taking his pills. We send new clothes down and the nurses make sure he changes his clothes and at least washes his face.

It's a sad case looking at my dad, but I suppose it gives me some motivation. Dad was talented and athletic but he chose to go down this path. It's hard to believe that the same man once did backflips from the highest diving board. I've seen first-hand the terribly damaging effects of alcoholism and a lack of self-love. I have learnt from him that life is about choices, and if you consciously keep making the wrong ones, ones that are damaging to your life, they consume you.

Now, if I realise I'm creating bad habits, I snap out of them fast. When you know in your gut that a certain behaviour isn't serving you well, you will feel anxiety, or unease. That's when I know a certain behaviour needs to change.

When I have a month where I go out and drink too much alcohol, I will feel less productive. My body and mind suffer, so I put myself on a drinking ban and look after my health and fitness. It doesn't mean I can never go out and party and have fun with my friends, it's just about keeping everything balanced and not tipping the scales so far in the wrong direction that it's hard to pull back from.

CHAPTER EIGHT

Ex on the Beach

I left Italia Conti with no job lined up, no prospects, absolutely nothing. Although it hadn't been diagnosed at the time, I was riddled with post-traumatic stress disorder, from the horrible things I saw in my childhood. A deep depression hit me. I was eighteen and lost. I didn't want to be alive any more.

Mum had lost her eyesight and was dealing with her own battles. Life was just not what I imagined it to be. I'd lost my drive; I had been so determined to be an actress. Now that I was away from the stage school buzz, I missed it so much. I missed being able to devote my life to things I loved, and now I was without that feeling. I didn't know who I was or how to behave. I felt like a total failure.

On my last day at Italia Conti, I saw the principal of the school, Anne Sheward. I went to the office and we both agreed that it was time I left. I had a lot to deal with and I couldn't do my best on the course with everything that was going on. My mum needed me and there wasn't any other decision to make.

How had life gone so wrong? I had left the school I loved, walked away from my full scholarship in my second year at Italia Conti, abandoning my dreams. Every day I was so sad and scared about my mum. I couldn't just put on my happy face any more. Each minute was a struggle.

I get mad at myself when I think back to this time. I just wish I could go back to my younger self and help her heal and keep her dreams alive.

I would tell her to keep working hard and that everything is going to be okay.

Once I had left Italia Conti and was helping Mum to rebuild her life as a blind person. I wasn't earning money, which was a huge problem. But helping Mum was a temporary release from my own thoughts.

After a few months of going further down the rabbit hole of self-doubt and loathing, things got worse and worse, and I was feeling sadder and more lost than I ever thought possible.

One day I took a load of paracetamol and tried to end it all. It was a stupid thing to do. I regretted it instantly and my stepdad and Mum took me to hospital to get my stomach pumped. I knew this was a desperate cry for help, but the help didn't really come.

I spent most of my twenties in a severe depression but no one would have known this unless they were really close to me. I was always overly excitable and happy and silly around people—the clown, the funny one. However, a lot of people with depression are the same; they put on this mask for everyone on the outside.

With no money coming in I knew I needed something fast. That's when I started glamour modelling. I thought, if I couldn't get an acting agent, maybe I could get a modelling one. It was something I was desperate to do but I didn't have any better plan.

I knew a girl in the year above me at Italia Conti who had a modelling agent, so I applied to the same place, and they suggested I put a portfolio together. I found photographers online who were starting out in the industry so I got my photoshoots for free. I sent the agent my portfolio and they took me on.

I was such a different person back then, starting out in the modelling world. I had lost sight of my dreams and was going out drinking and having fun which numbed the pain of that. I didn't want to deal with my issues. I was never embarrassed about being naked or being in my underwear, but it wasn't exactly a thrill either. It just felt like a means to an end.

At about the same time I started working at the racetracks. I had met other girls in the modelling industry who worked as racetrack girls and they helped direct me to the people who booked the models. Being a Maxxis Tyres grid girl was a fun distraction. I got to travel around the UK, starting different races and dressing up. I got to spend a week in the Isle of Man at the TT races and had a blast. However, the novelty eventually wore off. It was just a job that came at the right time. I wasn't living my dreams and I wasn't pushing myself towards them.

I started modelling for lads' mags such as *Nuts*, *Zoo* and *Loaded*, and appearing in newspapers like *The Daily Star*. This was a guise, I guess; it made the people around me think I was doing well. It gave me a sense of being a 'someone' instead of dealing with the fact that I felt like a failure.

I was earning okay money, but I knew it was a temporary career move. After doing it for a few weeks I started to worry it was potentially damaging any acting career I may have in the future. I didn't want people to search my name online and just see me as a girl at a racetrack, or a girl with her boobs out in a magazine. I had some fun moments, and I especially enjoyed shooting for *Zoo* magazine—they had a great team and I always felt happy and safe around people on set.

I met some wonderful people in the industry; girls with similar stories to me. I have always been so interested in the people who chose the same career path as me. A lot of (but not all) girls I met in the modelling industry had hard upbringings and issues with parents. I saw this as a pattern with the models. It made me wonder if the glamour world, for some, was a place for us to get validation and feel loved by the people reading the magazines.

It also led to my first proper TV appearance as a Sugar Hut Honey on *The Only Way Is Essex*. Being a Sugar Hut Honey was such a fun job; we got to go to the prestigious Sugar Hut nightclub in Essex each Friday and basically got paid to party. There were about ten of us altogether and we had to become the faces of the Sugar Hut, always dressed in orange, and at Christmas we would wear Santa suits.

There were some wild parties after these Sugar Hut nights. Everyone would head back to the club owner, Mick Norcross's, mansion and there would be dancing and more drinking. I didn't always go, but one particular time I got so drunk I thought streaking would be a great idea and jumped in a pond full of fish, even though the pond had frozen over. As you can imagine, I didn't try that one again so quickly after! The cold was horrific. I'm amazed I didn't die on the spot.

Although it was such an epic job, I was getting further and further away from my dream of becoming a working actress.

Every day I woke up not sure of what I was supposed to be doing with my life. I felt there was always something missing. I often say now that when we feel like that, it's because we are not living as our true selves. I thoroughly believe we are all born with a purpose and we just have to discover it. Usually you can find it when you feel utter joy in something you're doing. For me, it's performing and writing stories. I just didn't have the courage or self-belief back then.

I was stuck in a rut for most of my twenties. I put far too much effort into having a boyfriend and then I'd continue with the glamour modelling because I thought if loads of guys fancied me, surely my boyfriend wouldn't cheat and would always stay with me? This was not the case. In one particular relationship, after it ended with *me* being cheated on, the glamour modelling was used as a weapon against me. I was called a 'slag' and a 'cheap wank.' This just added to my self-loathing.

I felt that having a boyfriend must be the main goal in life and that it would surely make me happy, but it never did. God, I feel dumb when I think about those days!

I did have some fun times during this period; it wasn't all doom and gloom. Glamour modelling had its moments. I spent my twenty-first birthday with my close friends in a club in Mayfair in London, dancing on the bar with magnums of free vodka and shots of whatever we wanted all night. It kind of helped to be dating one of the younger owners who I had met on a previous night out. I quite liked him but he was such a player. That didn't last long, but the birthday party was super fun! He would take me to some amazing restaurants for dinner and exclusive parties. It was a life that was completely different to how I grew up.

I had many wild party nights in London, usually at the members' nightclubs where you'd need to know someone to get on the guest list.

Luckily, I always ended up knowing the right people and would regularly get a table in the clubs.

Often, I would just drive to the clubs. I had more fun staying sober and literally dancing my socks off to Hip-Hop and R&B. Sometimes I'd leave the car at home and stay at a friend's and get stuck into a night of drinking. I've always suffered from the worst hangovers though, and I've never remembered a night out being worth the headache the next day. I always much preferred being sober, so driving to see my friends and dancing was all I needed. I often (but not always) left the alcohol for other people.

I also liked to see how the other half lived. Those posh Mayfair clubs and fancy bars were something quite incredible to see. The clubs were often filled with footballers, sometimes the occasional Hollywood star. There was the odd occasion when a good-looker caught my eye. I'd try to get their number, go on a few dates, but that would be it. They were never the type I thought I would settle down with. I soon learned you didn't meet guys in that kind of club who were looking for anything serious, and the same can be said for the girls.

Once, a well-known American rapper was in a club and I was wearing white denim shorts with an American flag that caught his eye. He asked me to go back to the hotel after-party with his entourage, to which I replied, "Thanks so much for the invite, but I've heard stories of what goes on at rapper after-parties!"

He laughed and gave me a wink and I headed off home.

I used to go to really posh restaurants with my girlfriends—usually ones I had met from the modelling industry—and spend money I didn't have just so I could be part of the cool places to be. It was great food and they were amazing restaurants, but looking back now I think how stupid that was. I'd be broke for the next week just because I'd eaten some posh sushi! However, I don't regret it. I have great memories and I'm glad I got to experience it.

No one from my family questioned if I was happy or not. I was just left to my own devices; but I was never fulfilled by modelling and partying. I needed my career and to be creative, that was my happy place. That drive that I'd had when I was little—that got me a place at Italia Conti—was still inside me. I knew this wasn't what I was supposed to be doing with my life. That little girl who wanted to be an actress was still the person I really was deep down, and I had definitely lost touch with myself. The girl dancing in clubs seemed to be a different person.

I spent time working for Monster Energy from 2013 whilst modelling, as one of the world-famous Monster Girls. It was a badge of honour being a Monster Energy girl. They always had the coolest outfits for the promo girls. We were preened to perfection and would be invited to the coolest after-parties; we were paid to be there in our outfits just to keep the brand looking cool, young and fresh.

We would get to do photoshoots in hot tubs with MotoGP world champion, Valentino Rossi and be on stage with the Monster Energy DJs, dancing around, throwing t-shirts into the crowd with t-shirt guns. It was such a crazy and cool time.

I was fired as a Monster Girl a couple of times. I know that sounds silly as usually once you're fired that is it! However, I was re-employed a few times and still managed to mess it up, which was stupid of me. I couldn't go into work due to a hangover once and that didn't go down too well. It was a fun lifestyle, but you needed to be smart and composed at all times.

I was short for the typical Monster Girl, but they reminded me of the Amazonian women—awesome and hardcore—and I liked that image. It was fun, but so not me. To this day, in my heart of hearts, I'm a little geek and I embrace that now.

My first appearance on MTV's *Ex on the Beach* was aired in January 2015. I'm probably mostly recognised from this. It shows how much of an impact this show made at the time. It was a novel idea that totally threw people. What isn't interesting about putting a load of attractive youngsters together, letting them think they are about to find love and then, *wham*, in comes an ex to spoil it all? It was a crazy new concept that people loved.

Season Two had its fair share of dramas. Mine was with an ex called Rogan O'Connor. Rogan and I had met on holiday a few times and become good friends before we started to date, so it was a very short-lived 'thing' between us before we ended up on the show together. We are friends to this day.

For years after filming, Rogan would send messages telling me about how, when he would go on dates, women would come up to him at restaurants and tell him off for treating me badly on the show. In front of his date, they would tell him that he should be with me! This used to really make us laugh. I guess it showed that people had hugely invested in us as a couple.

Some people called us the 'Ross and Rachel' of reality TV. Which, in a way, I suppose we were. We had so many ups and downs on the show. There was never a dull moment.

When I first met the producers they had found me via Rogan—he was cast in the original eight. They would go on to the show before the exes started to arrive. I remember being called into the offices of the production company in London and having a chat with the producers about my life and how I was unlucky in love. I think they found my comic views on my shambolic love life quite funny.

After the initial conversation, I went back the following week to meet with the head of production at MTV, who would sign off on my inclusion in the show. I remember the meeting well. I was pretty damn nervous at the time because I really wanted to do this dating show. They didn't tell us it was *Ex on the Beach*.

After watching the first season with Vicky Pattison and Chloe Goodman I had an inkling of what it could have been, but they kept very quiet about what the show was called and kept trying to throw us off the scent.

I received a call about a week or so later telling me that I was part of the new series of a dating show. I was told when I would film my intro and I was given a date when I would be flying out of the UK to join the show, which was being filmed in a gorgeous villa in Marbella.

I had about two or three days to chill, meet producers and film little segments before I would be introduced to the rest of the cast in the villa. I was terrified. It finally dawned on me that I would be confined in a house with a load of strangers. All sorts of things were going on in my mind the night before my entrance. Would everyone like me? Was I on *Ex on the Beach*? If so, who would my ex be? My mind was in overdrive.

On the show, they always have the ex walk out of the water, all sexy, before being spotted by their ex-partner waiting patiently on the beach with two other cast members. However, it wasn't filmed like that. They would shoot the sexy walk out of the water before anyone was brought down to the beach. That way, they could get the perfect shot without wrecking the real reactions of your ex as they first see you materialise. They had to make sure that the reaction was raw and real. That's how they make it juicy!

So they filmed the water walk the day before. For the actual first scene I was held along the beach for a little bit, while the others (who had already joined the villa) were on their deckchairs facing away, so that they couldn't see what was happening. Then I was released to walk along the beach and into the scene. That bit was terrifying, but luckily my ex, Rogan, greeted me with a big hug. Although, I know now that he must have been extremely nervous as he was by that point seeing another girl on the show. He kept that quiet!

The one thing about filming these shows—that you don't get to see at home—is how utterly boring the days are. There were hidden cameras around the whole villa, but there were also film crews, so if drama kicked off, a group of people with their handheld cameras would run over to make sure they got the footage.

There was also a crew who would do our daily interviews. We would go off with them and talk into their camera whilst they asked us carefully formulated questions which fit the narrative of the episode they were filming. We would give our opinions, emotions and feelings about any of the situations going on in the villa.

When we were taken for our dates we would be loaded up into the van and transported to the location. While it was always great to get out of the villa to visit a new place for the dates, it took forever and we would be left in the van for hours whilst the crew set up the scenes. I was always so impatient back then and used to get really restless and fed up with just sitting in a van. I think that was the worst part of filming.

They reduced our alcohol intake at one point because one of the younger girls on the show got so drunk that she passed out and was throwing up! That sucked because "alcohol time" was always our fave. Since we were so bored all day and had to wait around, our nightly alcohol supply kept us going. It definitely made better TV when we were half-cut!

One night, we got to go to a nightclub for filming. I thought it meant we would see other people, but instead we were led to the top section of a club which was just for us lot to film in. I was drinking heaps of shots with Rogan. At that point we were totally joined at the hip and on a show like that, just having someone you know from outside of this experience was so comforting. Behind the back of the production crew we even sneaked Sambuca from the barman and by the time we left I was absolutely shit-faced, to put it bluntly.

When we got back to the villa I was absolutely off my rocker and ran straight inside, stripped off and jumped stark naked into the pool. Rogan quickly followed, stripping off and leaping in. He quickly realised that I was probably going to drown so he scooped me up and put me into bed. We were both so drunk we thought we had outsmarted the cameras because we'd stayed under them, and had sex. Sex was something I swore I'd never do on TV.

When I woke up I originally forgot that we had. When I realised that we slept together on TV, I felt shit. I was so mad at myself and worried that I'd let my family and friends down, but I couldn't do anything about it. It was too late. I just wallowed in, what to this day is up there with one of the worst hangovers of my life. I'm pretty sure I was still shit-faced for a good few hours after I woke up and the footage seems to back that theory up.

One of the clips people loved and still talk about is when I went for breakfast that morning looking like I had been hit by a bus. I couldn't stand upright and fell backwards over the breakfast bench.

Something you won't have seen on TV was that I had to ask the production team to get me a tin of baked beans and I sat and ate them cold for about an hour, just trying to keep them down. After that I was laying down behind the sofa.

Charlotte Crosby helped hide me as I napped by putting a blow-up crocodile over me. If the crew catch you napping in the day, they wake you up, and I was in no fit state to be disturbed. All in all, it was not a good morning for me.

I was surprised that there was not a huge backlash from the public or media after the sex scene aired. I think MTV viewers were used to these kinds of antics. Luckily, people seemed to brush over it. I think now, similar shows such as *Love Island* have stopped airing the sex scenes and I fully back that decision. Being penalised forever for something you did in your late teens and twenties isn't great and I don't think it should be shown on TV.

I remember when Charlotte Crosby and Gaz Beadle arrived in the villa. They had so much success and popularity from MTV's *Geordie Shore* that everything became a bit surreal. At the time of filming, I didn't realise how big *Ex on the Beach w*as going to be. It was massive.

I know some Love Islanders have spoken out about how filming worked for them on the ITV show and I think our experience was similar. 'Reality TV' is a kind of loose term in my eyes. There is nothing real about being put in a villa with a bunch of strangers, or your exes, and having no communication with anyone else. Automatically people will behave differently anyway.

Something that in the real world might make you a tiny bit cross would send you completely loopy in the villa. Usually, you can walk away from a situation and phone your friends or family and vent it out in order to deflate the situation. In the sheer boredom of some days in the villa, you'd sit and stew on it. Then if a producer noticed that you were slightly wound up, they'd ask about it in the video pop-up sections. This reminded you of the situation again and would make you more angry.

If you hadn't completely lost your head about it by then, the producers would say something along the lines of, "Jess, go over there and speak to (whoever) about this topic."

This would spark another confrontation, and then *BOOM*, a full-blown row would erupt about something you weren't really that arsed about when it happened. So you'd often see sides of yourself (and others) that weren't characteristic.

Nonetheless, I had the time of my life on my first season of *Ex on the Beach*. I really enjoyed the break of being away from real life for a while with no responsibilities, and was grateful for meeting new people on the show, and the whole experience. I was lost before that series, and it gave me a new career and opened up many doors.

A few years later, I spoke out on the *Victoria Derbyshire* show about how I felt let down by the production company behind *Ex on the Beach*. It wasn't made clear that I was talking specifically about the second time I went on the show.

It was Season Five, the All Stars series. That time around I felt it was so cut-throat. I didn't have a nice feeling about it from the minute I entered the villa. There was a huge amount of pressure to be more aggressive and angry and to just 'get with' boys as quick as possible to make better storylines.

Because of this pressure, I simply couldn't be myself and ended up with a really bad bout of anxiety I couldn't shake off. This was especially true after one of the producers, during the first or second night, said, "Lots of shagging tonight please, girls."

That didn't sit well with me at all. I know one of the other girls, a friend, ended up making a formal complaint about it. I asked to leave the villa early. I don't think I was even in there a full week. People could tell that I wasn't happy or enjoying myself and I knew it was best for me to leave. I was sad because my first experience of the show was great and I thought that was what I would be going back to.

I'll always hold Season Two of the show in high regard. Yes, I did have drunk sex on TV, hidden under my bedcovers, which Rogan and I have since worried for years and years about. But once you accept your mistakes, you can then take the lesson out of them, and I think that's what being human is all about.

I'm learning from my mistakes. I used to beat myself up about it for so long because I thought I had messed up any chance of a career after that. Truth be told, you can change things with hard work; not just in a chosen career path but also by working on yourself as a person. Mistakes don't have to define you.

To quote the former Girls Aloud singer Cheryl, "I've learned so much from my mistakes. . . I'm thinking of making some more!"

MTV gave me a platform. A fan base of some awesome and kind people, and I made some great friends and memories that I will cherish forever.

In my mid-twenties I realised there was more for me than what I was achieving. I had been on reality TV like MTV and hardly earned a penny. A funny thing I've learnt whilst doing these shows is that people think you've made it. But you're hardly paid anything, and at the same time you're forced to keep up an image that you're doing really well.

Most of the people I've worked with in reality TV are struggling to keep their heads above water. It really isn't all it's cracked up to be. You're just another self-employed person trying to make a living. You suddenly get a huge hit of fame, but don't get paid a huge amount of money and then have to keep up an image to stay relevant on a limited budget. It's awful.

Depending on how people behave on these shows, it can be hard to go back to normal employment. The problem I faced whilst filming these shows was feeling like I letting the producers down. So often in your heart you know a certain behaviour isn't going to serve you well, but you get encouraged by producers to act a certain way because they're after better TV. You end up doing things you don't necessarily think are right, but you also feel like you need to live up to the person who booked you on the job. It can leave you in a really low place. You don't know what you're supposed to do with your life. You become a different person.

Even robust, strong, thick-skinned people struggle to cope. In the space of nine months, from 2018 to 2019, there were two suicides of people who had been on reality TV shows.

This year, instead of watching *Love Island*, I decided to spend that one hour a day doing something productive like writing a book, reading and creating. *Love Island* is on every day for eight weeks. That's fifty-six episodes. Fifty-six hours of doing something productive and creative with my life. It feels good. I have no issue with people watching the show—it can be great entertainment—but I needed to manage my time better and I saw an opportunity in missing the show: the amount of hours I freed up for myself.

Also, I like to watch a good drama on the TV in my downtime these days, mainly because I like to see how the actors are portraying their characters. I can learn from them and put new skills into my character work.

Having been on reality shows, I always end up feeling sorry for the people involved. It makes it hard to watch. Not because a free holiday away with new and interesting people is bad, but because of what is waiting for them once they leave. If you're not a strong person, seeing the negative and horrid things on social media can be soul-destroying. We've all made mistakes in our lives, but if you go on one of these shows the press will dig it up and really try to destroy your character.

I stumbled into reality TV and was out of it as quickly as I was in it. However, it did give me a platform and got me back on track to my true dream of becoming a working actress. Also, with everything that's happened with my mum, I've always had such a strong sense of what's important in the world, like kindness and helping those who are less fortunate than ourselves. I'm able to see the bigger picture and therefore not get too bogged down with something so menial as reality TV and what people thought of me. So, for that, I am so thankful.

CHAPTER NINE

Falling In and Out of Love

It was 2015. I'd recently been through a horrible break-up and one night I was at home, bored, and thought, *The next good-looking guy who follows me on Twitter, I'm going to follow him back and send a smiley face emoji.*

A few minutes later, I got a notification to say I had a new follower. His name was Denny and he was a rugby player. He was cute, so I thought, *Why not?*

I followed him back and sent him a blowing-kiss emoji in a direct message. We started to talk and I liked this guy's vibe; he was funny. He was giddy that he had been watching me on MTV and now he was talking to me on Twitter. Although he made out for a while that he didn't know who I was or what I did—even though he had found me on social media first!

I played along, pretending I was a scientist for NASA! If he wanted to play, I was playing back.

At the time, *Ex on the Beach* was on MTV and was starting to get popular. People really liked it. I was getting recognised in the street and going to parties and being followed by paparazzi. I was always a geeky girl at school so this was so exciting. It was validation that I craved. I loved people constantly asking if they could get a picture with me and I think Denny liked the novelty of texting a reality TV star.

Denny and I met up. I drove to a place called Castleford in Yorkshire, where he was living, because he played rugby league Castleford Tigers.

Denny was a bit of a rugby hero there. I went there for the day but ended up staying a whole week.

On our first date, Denny was such a gentleman. We had many open and beautiful conversations. I told him all about my ex who had cheated on me and how painful that had been. He told me the same had happened to him and he was worried that he would struggle to trust anyone again. I felt we really connected on this. I started to see a future with him.

I've had some bad relationships in the past and I knew this was different. I felt comfortable and confident in my own skin. I'd never really felt like that before. Denny made me feel safe.

For the first few weeks we were together, we went out partying and clubbing a lot.

One night out, he said, "I love you."

I got butterflies and said it back. After such an awful previous relationship it felt amazing to have someone tell me they loved me.

It wasn't long till we were boyfriend and girlfriend. I was spending all my time in my car going up and down the A1 to see him. It took about four hours each way, so after three months of dating and falling for each other, we decided it would make sense to rent a place together.

It was a hard decision to move up north. My reality TV career was really getting started. I was getting lots of exciting offers and invitations for big events in London. So much of the reality TV industry is based down south, but I really wanted to be with him. I just knew that he and I were meant to be together.

You know when there's an instant connection with someone? It's so powerful that you can't ignore it. Your heart beats fast and you have goosebumps that zap and ping. Planets align. You're smiling all the time. You know the feeling, right? It's so perfect. We were in love and wanted to spend all of our time with each other.

After renting for a while we went on to buy a house together in Pontefract in Yorkshire. I was so far from my family and friends in Surrey. Everything was happening so fast but I didn't mind, I was a girl in love.

Denny's family originates from Samoa and soon after moving into our new home, Denny got a call to play rugby league there. I had never felt so proud. This meant so much to him. We stayed in a beautiful hotel in

Samoa and would lie together on the sunbeds, looking out at the most stunning ocean. I went to watch him play rugby and cried in the stand watching him do the national dance, which is called the Siva Tau. I was so, so proud. I thought, *That's my man!*

After the rugby we stayed out in Samoa to make the holiday last as long as possible. I had a bit of inheritance from my Grandad Sid and was also earning off the back of MTV, with brand endorsements and so on, which meant I had money in my bank. He was earning money too, but rugby league is significantly lower paid than rugby union and other sports. His career was doing well and he loved playing rugby.

We left Samoa and headed out to New Zealand and stayed in the most awesome places, visiting spas and doing so many fun activities. I even did a bungee jump and Denny filmed it. I am petrified of heights, but after I jumped it was all worth it.

When we returned from the trip, Denny started having trouble at his rugby league club with contract stuff. He ended up moving to a rugby union side just outside Manchester called Sale Sharks. This was a big deal, but Castleford Tigers fans were pretty unhappy that he had left. He had a big following there.

He got some terribly abusive messages on social media but so did I. I think his fans blamed me for the move. I was an easy target—the reality star girlfriend—but it didn't matter to me whether we lived in Yorkshire or Manchester or even on the moon. I just wanted him to be happy; I couldn't have cared less whether he played rugby league or rugby union.

I was called a 'slag' and much worse every day for months. I don't know why people thought I had any control over what he was doing with his career. They somehow thought I had demanded that he move clubs—like I had that power!

Denny going to Sale Sharks seemed like a good move and I was happy he was following his heart. Denny had started his career in rugby union, so it felt natural for him to return to it. I supported everything he did. I was as proud of his career as any of his fans. I had to learn to get used to all the abuse. Sports fans can be pretty brutal. I would say worse than the media, because at least you don't get death threats from the Sunday newspaper!

Moving clubs meant moving house again, so we moved out of our Pontefract house and rented it out. Sale Sharks found us a property to rent for six months, whilst we were looking for a new house to buy, near Manchester.

Just before we moved in, Sale Sharks paid for a holiday for me and Denny to go to Las Vegas. We had dinner at Casa Di Amore, a stunning Italian restaurant where Frank Sinatra (who I love) always used to go. They had a live singer singing Frank's songs and Rat Pack songs, and after dinner, by the incredible Bellagio water fountains, where choreographed fountains perform in time to lights and music, Denny proposed to me.

"Yes!" I said straight away.

I had never felt happier. Everything was so, so perfect and we looked out at the fountains, our arms round each other, and neither of us could stop smiling. As we kissed, we heard Frank Sinatra songs sweeping in with the breeze on the most perfect evening of my life.

The next day we went straight to the Little White Chapel and that's where we got married. It was me and Denny against the world and we would always be okay because we had each other. We hadn't told anyone that we got married except my mum and stepdad. We knew everyone would be angry because they couldn't be there with us and we didn't want to upset anyone, which backfired because everyone was more angry that we kept it a secret for so long.

It was only whilst I was in the *Celebrity Big Brother* house that it actually came out in the press. Before I went into the house I told my closest friends and Denny's family, as I knew there would be a chance of it coming out. The papers went wild with it with headlines such as *'Jess Impiazzi is secretly married to England rugby star Denny Solomona.'*

Once I was out the house and people knew we were having issues, the press ran a story saying Denny could be booted out the country if we divorce. It was a lot to deal with and really annoying having everyone speculate about our marriage. However, I was aware that going on these shows can be very intrusive to your private life. I just didn't realise how much I'd struggle to deal with it all.

Denny's career was going well and he'd got on to the England team. He was on an England tour of South Africa. I was at a friend's wedding and he was flying home the next day. I was beside myself with excitement to see him. As soon as he was home, I jumped into his arms and we went straight upstairs. I remember him asking me to take my contraceptive implant out as he had been wanting to start a family.

We would take a trip to Australia once a year for about a month when his rugby season ends, to spend time with his family who live there. Denny had family in Melbourne, New Zealand and Samoa. He had a really large family. I suggested that when we got back from our trip we could start trying for a baby, but deep down I think I knew I wasn't ready for this next step.

I had booked a car-drifting day for us, through a friend of mine, the day before we flew to Australia. It was a welcome home treat to say well done on his tour. I noticed Denny was a little touchy about everything and more moody than usual. I just put it down to him being tired. I'd seen him play rugby and it's such a brutal, physical sport—he always came back so tired and bruised, and playing for England was a big new thing for him.

The next day we flew to Australia. We had three weeks in Australia planned and then a five-day holiday in Dubai together and I was so excited to spend time with my husband. As we flew over there, everything seemed okay and I realised I didn't have anything to worry about. I was happy and relaxed and in love. Even though the whole relationship had certainly not been plain sailing, like any relationship, I'd met the guy that I felt safe with.

On our second night in Australia, we were staying at his eldest sister's house. I woke up in the middle of the night after a dream that Denny had cheated on me. My heart was pounding and something inside me told me to check his Instagram account. It was such a powerful realisation that something was wrong.

I looked at his Instagram and my world as I knew it got ripped to shreds. That sinking, brutal, unbearable feeling—you know the one where your legs go to jelly and your body goes ice-cold? I read a message from a South African girl and it was clear they had slept together—twice.

I ended up speaking to her over the phone and she told me everything! Maybe a little too much. Denny told her he saw a future for the two of them. When they met up he placed a ring on her engagement finger and said he wanted them to have children together. Even though he had just met her in a nightclub, they had unprotected sex before he kicked her out of the hotel room.

The worst thing is thirty-six hours later he had come home to me and we had unprotected sex and he was asking me to have his children! I felt immediately sick once I got all of the information, like my world was crumbling around me. I don't think, even to this day, that I've ever felt so alone, scared and heartbroken. I couldn't believe Denny had done this to me. I thought we had a strong relationship and I would never dream of hurting him like this.

That kind of betrayal is hard to get your head around. It wasn't just the cheating that hurt; he had told this girl he saw a future for them, even though I was at home, married to him. He had unprotected sex with her and didn't get himself checked or tested—he could have given me anything. The lack of regard for my health told me everything I needed to know. Denny had no respect for me.

I woke Denny up. I asked him if he had anything to tell me. Immediately he looked panicked and guilty, but he said no, there was nothing. The panic on his face spoke volumes. I asked him to follow me into the garage to tell me the truth. We were staying at his sister's house and I didn't want to wake her, her husband or their baby up.

"Denny, I know about the girl you had sex with in South Africa. Now tell me the truth."

I could feel my own heartbeat smashing against my chest. I was praying it was a lie. I was praying he would tell me it wasn't true, but in my gut I knew what was coming.

"Denny, look me in the eye and tell me the truth."

He kept his head down and wouldn't look up at me, then eventually muttered, "Yes. It's true. I'm sorry."

My legs wanted to give way. Every horrible thing I'd ever experienced in my life came flooding back to me. Every rejection, every broken heart and every tear I'd cried as a little girl found a way of re-entering my body.

I couldn't control the tears that raced down my face. My PTSD, flight or fight mode kicked in and I walked into the bedroom and started packing my suitcase.

Denny went and woke his sister up and told her what he had done and that I had found out. She came in to check I was okay. It was the early hours of the morning and she was just as gobsmacked as me by the information. I was packing and crying and shaking terribly. I felt like I was spinning; I was trying not to throw up. The one person who I thought I was safe with and felt at home with was gone. I couldn't believe it was happening, the person I'd married, the man I had dedicated the rest of my life to, had done this to me.

Denny's sister drove me to Melbourne Airport at about four o'clock in the morning and I checked in to the hotel there. I couldn't believe what was happening. As quickly as we'd fallen in love, he had ruined everything, and now I was in a strange airport on my own.

Even with this betrayal, I prayed he would come running after me, but he didn't. I just sat there on my own. I got into bed, took five Diazepam and downed all the vodka in the minibar, because I didn't know what else I was supposed to do.

But then somehow, things got much, much worse. . .

I'm still a big kid at heart. Here I'm getting a cuddle from Beetlejuice at Universal studios in LA. I spent a lot of time here. It took my mind off the divorce and felt like my sanctuary.

Top left: My dad Colin with me and my brother Joe.

Top right: My nephew Charlie with his mum Laureen.

Bottom: Family Christmas after we lost my Grandad. Left to right is my cousin Mikey, Uncle David, my mum, across the table my cousin Alex, Auntie Susan, my nan and me.

Top left: Me and Liam Payne in a nighclub, Funky Buddha, which was my fave place in my early twenties.

Top right: With Denny outside The Little White Wedding Chapel after saying our vows.

Bottom:. My dad Colin after I had just taken him for a hair cut!

Top: Me and Alex celebrating our Kilimanjaro success.

Bottom: The porters of Mount Kilimanjaro helping me promote my first stint on *Ex on the Beach*.

Top: I'm a big Harry Potter fan!

Bottom: On location in Los Angeles. Left to right, Luke Goss, myself and our DOP Vinnie.

Left: Me, Maggie Oliver and Ashley James out for dinner after *Celebrity Big Brother*.

Below: On the set of *The Seven* movie. Left to right is Rob, Amber, Luke, Josh and me.

Right: Myself and Kimberly Wyatt from The Pussycat Dolls. We star in the movie *RIA* together.

Below: The day after I got home from LA, I ran the London Landmarks Half Marathon to help raise money for Guide Dogs. Left to right is Ada, who was a producer on *RIA* the movie, Charlotte, my make up artist, myself and Rachel.

My mum, Debbie, and me, when we lobbied parliament with The Guide Dogs for the Blind Association to enforce stronger fines and penalties for taxi drivers who refuse to take Guide Dogs.

CHAPTER TEN

The End of a Marriage

While I was drinking vodka with Diazepam, Denny was on his way to New Zealand to see his mum. He clearly didn't care how I was feeling. There was no phone call and no text message. That hurt terribly; the person who I thought was a strong presence in my life was really just a coward.

The next morning, I felt awful. I don't know whether it was the tablets, the alcohol or the sadness, but I had such an unpleasant, restless night and was unable to sleep. I phoned reception to book another night in the hotel. I couldn't face leaving the room. I still hadn't processed what had happened.

I stayed in the hotel at Melbourne Airport for three nights without leaving the room, and I didn't sleep once. I tried doubling up on prescription sleeping pills and Diazepam but still didn't drift off. My body was in total and utter shock. My legs were still as wobbly as that moment when I'd realised what he'd done.

Looking back now, I shouldn't have been even a tiny bit shocked about what happened. Denny had shown me throughout our whole relationship that he was untrustworthy.

One of the things Denny and I first bonded over was that we had both been cheated on, but I found out his ex-girlfriend had never cheated on him. It was the other way round. He'd cheated on her and she was loyal to him.

When I confronted him about it, he admitted he had lied. I was dumbfounded. I couldn't believe he had fabricated a story to play on my emotions, trying to empathise with me. It was a manipulative thing to do and I was so insecure, so desperate for a man to love me and make me whole again that I let this huge red flag go.

Only now do I realise that being whole can only ever start with you. No person or thing can or should ever be your source of feeling complete, because if it's taken from you, you're incomplete again. You must be whole by yourself to attract the right people into your life, then you won't tolerate the red flags from the beginning.

Before Denny's South Africa trip, and a few months before I went into the *Celebrity Big Brother* house, Denny and I had another huge row where once again he had been dishonest about what he was doing when he was supposed to be in the England rugby camp. He went on a night out and ended up in a strip club, returning at stupid o'clock the next morning. He was kicked off the team and sent home.

The night before this happened, he'd sent me a text saying he was going to bed. Denny had no problem with telling bare-faced lies to me, I soon figured out. He phoned me in the morning, saying the England head coach was sending him home as he had a bad back.

I thought, *that's odd, why didn't they just give him physiotherapy?*

But I looked forward to him coming home and didn't question it. I drove to the gym and as I parked up I got another call.

"Jess, I've done something stupid," he said. "I've been kicked off the team. I went out last night and the boss found out."

I was so disappointed in him. I just hung up. I didn't have anything to say. When I found out where he'd been and how much money he'd spent, I just found it pathetic. I packed my stuff and left. I went home to my mum's to clear my head for a while.

They do say love is blind. I'd turned a blind eye to any doubts that I'd had, but now I realised I'd been right about everything. Maybe that was why I couldn't sleep. I was replaying every moment of our relationship and re-evaluating everything he had ever said or done.

I couldn't stay in the hotel any more. It was making me more miserable. I still had a week to go before my flight back home—because of the flights that Sale Sharks had booked for us, I couldn't just jump on a plane back home the next day. I was glad as it gave me more time to process what had gone on. I was also scared to return to our home without him; it would have been so hard going back, not knowing what the hell was going on with my life. It would have made everything more real.

I ended up booking a separate flight to Sydney. I spent a week there before I'd have to fly back to Melbourne to catch the flight back to the UK. I'd been to Sydney before and my friend Scott lived there. I vaguely knew my way around the city.

I had to do something. I needed to find somewhere that was even a tiny bit familiar since I couldn't go home. I was now angry and determined to show Denny that I was worth more than what he had done to me.

For the first time in three days, I had a shower and got dressed. I remember cleaning my teeth in the mirror playing some feel-good Beyoncé songs and giving myself a pep talk in my head. I then packed my suitcase and went outside. I walked over to Melbourne Airport with my earphones in, listening to as many girl power songs as I could find and jumped on the plane to Sydney.

Once I arrived at the hotel in Sydney, I made a cup of tea and it was like drinking life back into myself; I hadn't had any nourishment and that one cup of tea just helped me feel a little bit more normal.

On my second night in Sydney, I went out for the evening. I didn't even know how to behave anymore. I was just trying to get through the days. I hadn't eaten for about four days. I was just smoking and drinking Pimm's for breakfast, lunch and dinner.

As well as Scott, I knew a few other people in Sydney—mutual friends of mine and Denny's. I was invited to a party by the mum of one of Denny's rugby friends. I got drunk and it just felt so weird. I had no idea where I was or what was going on in my life, and I didn't want to talk to anyone or for anyone to look at me, so I left the party early. I drank more in my hotel and then I lost it. I was sobbing uncontrollably. I looked at myself in the mirror, and hated what I saw: a pathetic, ugly loser.

No wonder my husband cheated on me. I'm nothing. I have nothing going for me.

All I knew was pain, so why the fuck was I even here? I'd sacrificed everything for him. I'd thrown it all away—my career, my happiness, my self-esteem. I'd made such a stupid mistake. I completely blamed myself. I'd messed everything up.

I started writing a text to Denny. I wanted him to know how I was feeling. I told him that I hated him and this was his fault and that I loved my family, and I was going to end it. I pressed send. I took about seven Diazepam and the rest of the sleeping tablets and passed out.

I got woken up in a shock by banging on my hotel door. It was Denny's friend's mum, who I'd been with earlier that night. I stood up, dizzy and cloudy-headed, and opened the door. A few minutes later the police arrived in my room with a paramedic, and I'd never felt smaller. I regretted sending that text and also felt pissed off and surprised that I'd woken up after taking those tablets.

I felt like such a dickhead. I never thought I'd be that person again. If I felt pathetic the night before, I felt ten times that now. What was happening to me?

The paramedics did some tests to check if I was okay and thankfully I was. I promised everyone that I didn't want to take my life, and that it was a big misunderstanding. I was just feeling very low after something that had happened to me. They left, along with Denny's friend's mum, and I just sat there, crying, on my own again. I felt dizzy all day after that, with the tablets working their way through my system.

Denny phoned my entire family and told them what I had done. I felt so terrible. I couldn't believe what I had put them through. I was such a long way from home. Now I had an extra emotion to carry around: pure guilt. I wish I had told them about how I was feeling. They knew what had happened and that I had left Denny, but I lied and convinced them that I was fine. I was far from it and I should have got help rather than act so stupid.

A couple of hours later, I got a message from Denny. He was on a flight, coming over to Sydney to take me back to New Zealand where he had been staying since I left Melbourne. However, I'd already organised for my friend Scott to come and see me for a few days, and it just so happened they were landing at the same time.

When I saw Denny, he hugged me. I felt conflicted. On one hand I hated him and didn't want him to touch me, but at the same time I felt safe and I never wanted him to let me go. I'd had so much love for him since the first time we'd met that it was inevitable that some remained inside me. Your brain can't get rid of love quickly.

I spent a few days with Scott, and invited Denny on a few trips. It was so hard. I wanted to hug him and forget about everything that happened but he had totally destroyed me. Funnily enough, Denny and I had actually been getting on okay and I truly thought maybe there was a way to fix this. We both booked ourselves on a flight back to Melbourne, as my flight home to England was the following day. He decided to fly with me back to Melbourne and when I left for England he would travel back to New Zealand.

It felt okay travelling together. Things started to feel. . . normal. We had drinks in the bar, and tried to discuss things and work out where we had gone wrong. I was so low that I wanted him to come home with me. I had lost about a stone in weight within ten days and was mentally and physically extremely weak.

That night, we got into bed and Denny fell asleep. The drunken paranoid me checked his phone. I saw that the whole time he was with me in Sydney, he had made another Snapchat account and messaged loads of girls, and lots of them were mutual friends of ours.

I flipped. He had seen what he had done to me, yet was still sneaking around behind my back! I threw water at him, which woke him up pretty quickly, and then I punched him in the face. I was screaming and crying. What had I done to deserve this? I always saw us as a team, a perfect couple and I realised we never were. I was just a stupid fool who loved someone so deeply, and clearly his words never matched his actions.

I was disgusted at myself for punching him. Who even was I anymore? I should have walked out of the hotel room and just never spoken to him again. I will always regret my actions. I had no right; it lowered my worth too. It is never acceptable to lay your hands on another human without consent and I'll forever be sorry about that.

The next day, I almost missed my early flight. I cried the whole journey home. Two older men were sitting in the seats nearby. When they saw me at the aeroplane bar, they asked if I was okay. I must have looked a right state. I told them I wasn't. I explained what had happened and what had gone wrong whilst crying my eyes out.

They were both fathers and one of them hugged me and said, "I promise you everything will be okay. You're worth more than that rubbish—it's his loss."

I went back to my seat and I put it down so it felt like I was on a bed. I lay there staring at the roof of the plane. The way he'd told me I was going to be okay played around in my head. They were the first positive, happy words I'd heard anyone say for a long time. I realised he was right. This little act of kindness from a stranger had helped more than anyone could know. I'd felt so lost and alone, and those kind words and that hug made me hold on to a bit of hope.

I fell asleep, and by the time I woke up again I was feeling okay. For the first time in days, I felt something vaguely close to the old me. It was going to take me a long time to get over Denny, but the men on the plane had reminded me that I was a fighter, and a good person, and this was just another setback. I was going to be okay.

Denny was a talented guy, but he didn't make very smart choices. I put my heart and soul into that relationship and I learnt some very valuable lessons. Words mean nothing if the actions don't match. I worked this out throughout our time together; eventually it was the reason we got divorced.

When the marriage finally came to an end, Denny and I only communicated via text or lawyers. We never saw each other again. He kept my dogs, my furniture, my TVs. The lot. I didn't have another place to live and had to move to my mum's whilst I figured it out. I gave away eighty percent of my belongings to the charity shop. It was a freeing experience, giving away my entire life. I could now start from scratch. I also saw it as a metaphor for the other areas of my life. A kind of lesson in letting things go.

One thing I found that really helped me through it was reading self-development books. I found a fantastic author and guide called Gabby Bernstein. Her book *The Judgement Detox* was a saving grace for me. It made me realise how much we judge others in life, either for how they behave or for how that behaviour makes us feel. I learnt that by letting go of the judgements for my ex-husband's cheating, I could let go of anger and hurt. I came to realise that no matter what had happened, it had, so why fester on something that no one could change by making him feel bad, or by sitting in my own thoughts?

In constantly judging him, I was keeping myself stuck in a horrible mindset. Once I released that judgement, I also found myself being less resentful. I lost the anger and I felt free. I really recommend that if you're in a state of anger towards someone, to check out that book.

I think divorce is a scary word. When you've built a life with someone, which is then ripped away, it's hard not to sink into the sadness of it. Especially if you really thought it was forever. Whenever anyone asks me about divorce now, or if they're going through the same thing, I often tell them it was the best thing that happened to me. Not because I'm being bitter and horrible to my ex-husband; actually quite the opposite. I say this because without the relationship, without the pain, without him, I would have been stuck.

I wasn't pursuing my dreams. I wasn't growing as a person and I wasn't being the best version of myself. Sometimes being totally ripped apart gives you a different mindset. The good thing about rock bottom is there's only one way up. A seed has to split before it becomes a tree.

Although divorce is awful it's the perfect time to find yourself again, to remember what you love and what passions you had before you were distracted by someone else. It's a chance to be authentically you again and to learn to love yourself for who you are alone.

Despite the bad things that happened with Denny, as well as with other boyfriends and the other horrible things life throws at so many of us, I'm lucky to have some great friends and family. My nieces' mum Laureen, my best friends Alex, Teagan and Jamie, and my mum and stepdad Jim are always there at the end of the phone if the shit hits the fan. That's how you know who your true people are. It's not in the good times you find out who is there for you; it's in the hard times. The people who will drop anything to come to you in your time of need. I treasure those people with all my heart.

CHAPTER ELEVEN

My Nan and Grandad

I know not all people are as fortunate as me when it comes to having the most wonderful grandparents. I'm so thankful that mine could play such a huge part of my life. They're home to me. I used to love it when my mum and I would stay with them. We would always have a home-cooked dinner made by Nan, and afterwards we would settle down in the living room. Everything about being there just felt safe. Even thinking about it now, I can taste my nan's cooking.

On Saturday nights we would sit down with bowels of ice-cream and watch *Gladiators*, *Man O Man* with Chris Tarrant, *Baywatch* and *Blind Date*. I used to absolutely love it, sitting there with everyone, laughing and joking. I think my family would have been great on *Gogglebox*!

Christmas throughout my early years until my late teens was always held there too. My aunt, uncles and cousins would come round. Me and my younger male cousins, Nick and Alex, would always play the best games at Nan and Grandad's house. We were desperate for Nan to buy us a trampoline for when we stayed over, and eventually she agreed. It was a great buy. The three of us were never off it. We would spend hours and hours on the trampoline. Nan and Grandad's house was the fun place to be. Plus Nan always cooked the most delicious food.

The three of us would always run around the house like crazy children, playing *Harry Potter*. We would get sticks from outside and use them as wands and hide from each other, or run from room to room shouting different spells. I only have wonderful memories of Nan and Grandad's house.

My grandparents from my mum's side of the family are Italian, and it's where my surname originates from. My grandad Mike was a black cab driver in London and had been for many years. He was half Italian. I was told that my great-grandparents came over to England and my great-grandad sold the best gelato in town.

My grandad would always have Tuesdays off work because that was his golf day with the lads, usually with Uncle David too. He loved his golf. As he got older, though, he couldn't play golf so much, so Tuesday became a rest day. Grandad didn't really ever retire; he worked on the taxis right up until his eighties! I loved him so much. He was a legend; a true gentleman.

One day, at home in Haslemere with Mum and my stepdad Jim, Mum got a phone call from my aunt. I must have been around twenty-one years old. I was sitting at the computer in our little flat.

"Jess, that was Aunty Susan," Mum said. "She's been with Nan and Grandad at the hospital for a check-up and they've found a shadow on Grandad's lung." She was trying to hold back her tears.

"What does that mean?" I asked.

"Potentially lung cancer," she said.

I burst out crying. Something in me knew there was going to be no good outcome from this.

A few days later, it was confirmed—Grandad had really advanced lung cancer. He was already in the last stages and it had spread around his body. I couldn't believe it.

He had to stay in the hospital. We were told it was terminal and there was only pain relief that he could have now.

He always loved cans of John Smith's beer and a KitKat Chunky on evenings when he was at home. Now that he was in the hospital, it wasn't going to change, not under my watch. We were told no alcohol, but if he was going to die I wasn't stopping him having what he wanted.

Every single day after my promo work or modelling, I would hide a beer and a KitKat Chunky under my jumper or in my bag. I would go up to my grandad's ward, pull the curtain back from around the bed and give it to him. You should have seen his face!

Later, Grandad was allowed to come home. My uncle converted the downstairs dining room into a bedroom for Nan and Grandad to sleep in so he didn't have to climb the stairs as he was too weak. He was so poorly, bless him, though he kept trying to pretend everything was normal; he didn't want us to be upset. He had drips in his arms, but he sat in his usual chair, clearly in pain, watching his programmes so we didn't worry. After a few days it got too much and an ambulance had to take him back to hospital.

He was transferred to the Princess Alice Hospice in Esher in Surrey, and the staff were amazing there. The care they gave to him and the other patients was so beautiful. I've always been so in awe of people who devote their lives to caring for others.

One particular day, I went to visit Grandad and I could see he was getting weaker. I'd been so strong, not letting any emotions in so he wouldn't see me sad, as I knew that would upset him. I needed a blow-out, so I went to Guildford with some of my friends and got so drunk. I tried to forget everything and have a really good night because it had been such a long time since I'd had any fun. Sometimes you just need a night like that.

The next morning, I was really hungover. I spoke to Uncle David, who had gone up to see Grandad, and asked if it would be okay if I didn't visit today. My uncle told me the nurse was quite happy with his stats; they'd gone up and it would be fine if I couldn't make it in. My uncle left without me and said he'd say hi from me and that I'd be back in the next day.

That night, I fell asleep and woke in the middle of the night. I shot bolt upright, tears streaming down my face. I'd had a dream that Grandad came in, kissed me on the forehead and then left this world.

My phone rang; it was Mum, in tears. "Jess. . . Grandad passed away a few minutes ago."

Mum had been staying at my nan's house so they were picked up by Uncle David and taken to the hospice. Laureen drove round and picked me up. When I arrived at the hospice, my Aunty Susan, two cousins Alex and Nick and my brother were there.

We went in and sat around Grandad. Holding his hand, I was heartbroken. We all were.

I fully believe to this day that my grandad came to me in my dream and said goodbye because he knew how sad I would be. My uncle told us that the last thing Grandad had said to him was for us to take care of Nan.

I struggled during my grandad's funeral. Mum and Jim had separated for a while. Mum had gone off to the Royal National College for the Blind and met a man who she ended up having an affair with. Eventually, Mum told my Jim and they separated.

I hate cheating, however, Mum and Jim had been under such strain and with Mum leaving home to be a resident at the Royal National College for the Blind, they lost that spark in their marriage. They didn't understand each other anymore, no matter how hard they tried. It was a horrible thing for them to go through, but luckily for me, Jim was there to stay and even when they were separated for five years, he still acted like my dad. I lived with him for a while and he helped me move house. Jim regularly took me for Sunday dinner. I heard a quote once, which I think is so relevant to our relationship: *'Stepdads are the best because they step up when real dads step down.'*

At Grandad's funeral, I had my boyfriend at the time, Davo, an Australian motorbike racer, with me. My whole family was together. Jim came on his own.

As we were lowering the coffin, Mum burst into tears and Jim welled up. I'd never seen him cry before. He had to walk off. I ran up to him and asked if he was okay and if he would stay longer, but he replied, "I can't, Jess. I just want to put my arms around your mum and comfort her, but I can't."

The wonderful thing is that after five years, Mum and Jim got back together! They ironed out the things that didn't work and they have their happily ever after.

I felt lost once Grandad passed away. I always knew my grandparents were there; my comfort blankets. If shit ever hit the fan, I knew I had Nan and Grandad. Now that comfort was gone.

Nan was struggling in the house by herself. She would make dinner each night forgetting that Grandad wasn't with us any more, then call one of us in tears because she'd waited for him to come home and then remembered. Soon after, Nan was diagnosed with dementia.

She went to live with Mum in a rented house in Haslemere so that she could be fully looked after. My mum was amazing. Being fully blind, it was hard for her to cope, but they got through it. My nan had a wonderful sense of humour. She would always be the life and soul of the party, dancing at every opportunity.

Once Nan was living with Mum, she started to enjoy a Baileys at night—just the one. Which was crazy because she was never a drinker. But it seemed to help her sleep, which she hadn't done properly since Grandad passed.

When I was still with my ex-husband, Denny, we spent a weekend at Mum's when we were visiting from Manchester. It was a Friday night and we were having a night in together. Nan wanted another glass of Baileys and Mum said, "No, Mum, no more tonight. I've got to get you to bed!"

Nan agreed, but then, knowing Mum couldn't see, she looked over at Denny and went, "Pssttt!"

Denny looked over and Nan winked at him and wiggled her glass. He looked panic-stricken. He was too scared to say no to her, but also too scared to get caught by my mum! I couldn't help, because I was laughing too much, plus I didn't know what to do either.

Mum finally worked out what was going on by the third "Pssttt" directed at Denny and I was in hysterics.

Nan was a funny old soul. She'd told me laughter is the best medicine, and I try to live by that rule today.

It was just after Nan's ninetieth birthday when she started to slip. Mum phoned me one day whilst I was living in Manchester with Denny, saying Nan had been picked up by an ambulance in the middle of the night. She'd tried to walk to the toilet and had fallen over; she couldn't get back up and Mum couldn't help. Mum couldn't see and it was quite a dangerous situation. She was really amazing during this time looking after Nan. It must have been so hard for her.

They took Nan to hospital that night as a precaution. She ended up staying in the hospital for a while. The doctors were worried about her lungs and they didn't think she was strong enough to go home with Mum.

Nan's dementia was getting bad. She would talk to us sometimes thinking we were the adults and she was the little child again. It was terribly sad watching her go through this, but we would try to go along with it as much as possible to make sure Nan felt safe.

Nan was in the hospital for quite a few weeks before everyone agreed that it was safer for her to be in the nursing home in Haslemere now that the disease had become quite severe.

Nan was always terrified about having to go into a nursing home. She never wanted that. However, we made sure it was close to us and a safe environment. Mum and I knew some of the staff and they would take great care of her.

We made sure at least one of the family would visit her daily and stay for hours. We would take shifts so that during the day Nan would never really be left without one of us. She was only there to make sure that at night-time she was safe, with staff to hand to help.

I was lucky that during this period I was able to spend a lot of time down at Mum's, rather than being with Denny in Manchester, as I had a small role in an independent movie that was being filmed down south. It meant I was staying at Mum's for a few weeks at a time. I'm so grateful for that. I love that I got to spend that extra time with my nan; another sign showing me the universe works in great ways.

I was taking my niece Lydia back up to stay with Denny and I for the weekend. I'd only been back up north for about an hour when Mum called and said Nan had died. I wanted to drive straight back, but Mum said it would be silly to do that and it would be better for Lydia to have a distraction.

Denny was at training and I was home alone with Lydia. I calmed her down, trying to hold in the tears, and I explained that something sad had happened and Nanny Kath was now in heaven. We both hugged for about twenty minutes, crying.

I texted Denny and he rushed home from training to look after both of us. No matter how our marriage ended and how messy it became, I'll always be thankful to Denny for this. He was a rock to me.

The day Nan passed away was one of the saddest days of my life. It was also the start of a big change. The grandparents, who I felt held us together were now gone.

I went to see Nan at the funeral home with Mum, Jim, my brother

Joe and Denny. She looked so beautiful, like the dementia had gone. She was in her white suit and looked at peace. My beautiful Nan. I gave her a kiss on the cheek and Denny cuddled me. Usually, in times of distress, due to my PTSD I'd need to be alone with no one near me, however I felt safe with Denny.

At Nan's funeral, I purposely wore the same butterfly-print dress I'd worn to Grandad's funeral. I read a poem like I did for my grandad and also for Charlie. At the end, we all placed a single yellow rose on top of Nan's coffin and she was cremated, to be laid to rest with Grandad.

My beautiful grandparents—the end of an era.

I learned so much about love and kindness from Nan and Grandad. The memories will stay with me forever and I truly believe that they both still guide me through life. In times of need, I often ask them for guidance and I believe that they've always pulled through for me.

CHAPTER TWELVE

Climbing Mountains

I was twenty-two, glamour modelling, not really fulfilling any dreams but hey, I was making money. Little did I know how much things were going to change for me. My phone rang and it was Mum.

"Jess, I'm going to climb Ben Nevis in Scotland with the charity Sight for Surrey and wondered if you wanted to do it with me to raise some money? They've helped me a lot with the gadgets they've sent me and it would be a nice adventure!"

I thought, *Wow, if Mum is planning to do* this *blind, I really don't have any excuse to say no!*

I really wanted to do something with my life. I wasn't feeling fulfilled with any part of it. Nothing was quite going the way I wanted it to, and I needed an adventure, a new challenge. I was drinking too much and living for the weekend, so it would also be a great way to buck up my ideas and clean up my lifestyle. I told her I'd love to join her, and started helping with fundraising.

A few weeks later, our rucksacks were packed and after a sleepless night we set off. We met Martyn, our mountain leader from Birmingham; probably the funniest man I've ever met. He was to become a firm fixture in my charity mountaineering quests to come. A group of us met at the charity's headquarters in Leatherhead in Surrey, and then jumped on our minibus for the long trip up to Ben Nevis. It was like going on a school trip; everyone was really excited.

Sitting in front of me and Mum was the head of the charity, Lance, a wonderful elderly man who used to be very high up in the RAF.

I was thrilled to be able to help such a cool charity. Sight for Surrey work with people who provide support to the blind and partially sighted community and have done since 1922. The difference they make to people's lives is phenomenal. I'll never get bored of doing things to help charities. It's something I'm so passionate about.

Mum and I checked into a hotel and got ourselves ready for the next morning when we'd start climbing. We had a nice meal in the hotel with the whole team and then went off to get an early night. We were woken up early by our alarms, got ourselves ready and then met the others in the hotel lobby before all jumping in the minivan to our starting point.

When we arrived at the bottom of the mountain, I pulled out my walking boots and Martyn almost had a heart attack. They were fresh out of the box, never worn. Any avid climber or walker knows you need to wear your boots in. Oops! He wasn't feeling confident that my feet would get me up the mountain without any pain or blisters but luckily for me I was fine—not a blister in sight at the end.

Mum couldn't make it the whole way up the mountain because it became a little dangerous. She went well over halfway and was super happy with that. I was so proud of her. I can't imagine how scary it must be climbing a mountain that you can't see. We took turns being her guide, but we didn't want any accidents, so Martyn took Mum back down the mountain to the pub where they would wait for us.

The rest of us continued up to the top and it was an amazing adventure. I, in true drama-queen nature, was certain a huge bird was trying to attack me as it followed me around the top of Ben Nevis. Everyone had a good laugh at me running and hiding from the bird circling above my head.

On the descent, Lance's knees buckled and he kept slipping and falling over, which was concerning me quite a lot. I was worried he was going to badly hurt himself. The others carried on at their fast pace, but I stayed behind with him. He told me he was fine, but I didn't want to leave him so I took his arm and slowly and carefully we made our way down together. The rest of the team and the mountaineer in our group had deserted us. It was getting dark and I started to panic. By now Lance was in agony and I wasn't certain of the way back. I decided to keep going and just stick to the path. We had our head-lights on and just hoped for the best.

I was pissed off with the rest of the group for leaving us, and when the group turned up at the pub without us, Mum and Martyn were furious. I think only then the rest of the group realised they shouldn't have left us on our own.

Martyn left Mum with the group and set off to find us. Luckily, Lance and I were making great progress in the right direction. I scared the life out myself a few times; it was pitch black, our little head-lights guiding the way. I could hear noises like little shuffles in the bushes next to me. I've watched far too many horror films, and after the bird incident I was certain our time was up.

I didn't admit to Lance that I was starting to get really scared, and I could tell he was nervous too. He kept apologising but I said it was fine, the two of us would make it, together. Me and Lance really bonded on that walk. We had some interesting conversations and Lance is such a positive person that for the first time in months I started to feel good about myself.

I turned my head to look in the bushes, and looking back at me were these glowing eyes. I felt like my scream was stuck in my throat. I was absolutely terrified.

Lance, the RAF tough guy, saw and explained to me in a sympathetic, kind way that there was no devil in the bush; it was just a sheep! You can imagine how embarrassed I was.

Out of nowhere, Martyn appeared from around the corner and found us. We were nearly back to safety. For the first time Lance and I admitted to each other how scared we'd been, and together we went back to the rest of the group. I was so glad to be back with Mum again.

The trip gave me the most wonderful sense that I was achieving something. I missed that feeling. It had been years since I had felt proud of myself. I hadn't felt like I'd really achieved anything since my Italia Conti days.

Not too long after, Martyn told me he was setting off on another trip soon, this time to Borneo to climb Mount Kinabalu.

"Do you want to come along for another adventure?"

I said yes immediately. I asked my best friend Alex if she wanted to come too. I had told her about the first trip and she was keen to try it for herself. The two of us started fundraising for the charity climb straight away.

Before we knew it, Alex and I were on a plane to Borneo, the largest island in Asia. Once we landed and checked in to our hotel, we had a day to be tourists and take in the beauty of Borneo.

I had been lucky enough to go to Borneo as a child with my Aunty Susan and my younger cousins Alex and Nick. My Aunty owns a travel company for meetings and incentive trips and has made it a great success over the years. When we went as children, we stayed in the best hotels and got to visit the orangutan sanctuary, which was simply amazing. Maybe not so much for the poor American guy on our trip, who had his balls grabbed by one of the orangutans! Then it stole his camera.

This time we were in budget accommodation as backpackers. I'd always wanted to backpack. There's something about it that I always found intriguing—maybe because it's a world away from how I usually travel.

The day we climbed the mountain can only be described as magical: the wildlife, the jungle and the local people. I love the change of scenery the higher you climb. I would always recommend a good mountain climb. It's honestly great for the soul. The rats were the funniest; they looked more like squirrels and could jump super high. One jumped at me during our sandwich break and stole it right out of my hand.

We reached the summit of the mountain; it looked more like the moon. We had to hold on to a rope at one point and pull ourselves across the big slabs of rock, in the pitch black with just a head-light to guide us.

I'm no good with heights, which sounds ridiculous seeing that I climb a lot of mountains, but as you climb up there is great support from your team, which keeps me going. I'm one of those people who has to beat their fear, so even though I was terrified of heights I would reassure myself and just keep powering on, but this particular part was horrid. You had to use the ropes to hold on and get from one ledge to another. Alex was shouting reassuring words to me and staying close by. The ledge was only wide enough for my little feet. I was crying, tired and worn out, but I realised I could either carry on or be stuck there for life.

Good old Martyn, the mountain leader, thought I was joking and shouted, "Get a move on, Jess," which made me cry even more.

He felt terrible when he realised how scared I was. I got over it quickly though. You have to when you're somewhere like that. You feel a long way from home and being scared doesn't help anyone. You need to conserve your energy for walking.

Even though mountain climbing is super hard and it takes a lot of mental strength to get to the summit, it's one of my favourite things to do. You have a mixed group of people from around the world and you get to meet people you'd never normally meet and hear their stories. Everyone is doing these trips for different reasons. It can be for charity, or in memory of someone they've lost, or even just to find themselves. I think it's beautiful when people go on their own, climbing for no other reason than to set themselves a challenge.

For this very reason I agreed to climb Mount Kilimanjaro. I knew that mountain would be a tough one, but I was so excited. I think I was starting to get addicted to mountains!

It was a long trip over to Africa. We had to catch a flight from London to Ethiopia and change for our next flight to Addis Ababa. Again, we had Martyn as our leader, alongside a lovely experienced climber named Darren. Alex was there too, by my side yet again, and a few other English people. The rest of the group were Americans. We also had our team of porters, who were locals from Kilimanjaro, and they helped us with our bags and with setting up tents and cooking food for us. They really were incredible.

I have the most beautiful memories of our porters. Our head porter "Whitey" always made sure we were okay. At every campsite the porters would keep our moods up, singing traditional African songs mixed in with some current R&B, and we would dance all night.

I love seeing people come together. We see so much sadness and separation and hate in our media outlets and on the news, but doing things such as mountain climbing, where strangers all come together to help each other gives me a special feeling. It's during these times when you see the beauty in life, and know it really is worth it.

When you climb mountains, you quickly become close with your team members; you become a family. We helped each other and encouraged each other, shared snacks and energy supplements in times of need. It was great. A real cool team. Like so much in life, in mountain climbing you're reliant on the people around you.

You lose all modesty and vanity. When you find out the toilet situation up the mountain, and you have to deal with a little hole dug in the ground, where you have to hover—hoping for the best—you soon learn what's important in life! You can hear everything. It's so embarrassing!

My tips for if you ever climb a mountain are:

1. Don't forget your baby wipes.
2. Make sure you bring proper footwear.

I like to climb mountains not just to raise money for charity, but also because it keeps me going, mentally. I look at life sometimes the way I saw Mount Kilimanjaro. Standing at the bottom, I thought there was no chance I was getting up all the way to the top. It was way too big; I was scared and daunted. I was so tiny compared to this ginormous mountain. However, once I started I got excited. No matter how hard it got or how long it took, just by putting one foot in front of the other, I made it. I like to see that as my metaphor on life.

That's how I know I'll always fulfil my dreams. I'll get there, with just one foot in front of the other. If you're ever feeling a bit stuck or sad or fed up, I really hope you'll think of signing up to some kind of charity walk, climb or adventure. It's such an important thing to do. You get to meet incredible, funny, inspiring people and your worries seem such a long way away. Sometimes taking yourself out of your comfort zone can help you find your way in life.

Kilimanjaro was one of the hardest things I've ever done, but one of the most rewarding. I have the best memories. One of my favourites was sleeping in a tent for seven nights, and it got so cold at night-time. I was sharing with Alex, and you would think we would be moaning about how cold and uncomfortable it was but we loved it. We would spend each night laughing and talking.

Alex and I have such a funny friendship. On one level we are complete opposites—Alex is smart and logical and I'm irrational and eccentric—but the friendship works, and we bring out the other side to one another.

We always say if anyone who didn't know us heard our ridiculous conversations we would be locked in padded cells! We love to pretend we're blasting out great songs and that we're Whitney Houston, but singing as out of tune as you can get. Usually just in the car, but sometimes we will do this in public and obviously get some very funny looks. We did this a few times in our little tent. Some didn't like it, but it certainly kept us entertained.

We were so cold we would try to sleep in the same sleeping bag some nights. A yoga mat really wasn't any help as a mattress, so every few minutes we would have to try to move our numb areas and we'd end up getting trapped and entwined around each other. We were exhausted but it was still funny.

I liked to moan and make jokes with Alex and Martyn the whole way up the mountain to keep us entertained. Some of the others didn't quite approve of this and got moody with us. In the end they isolated themselves from the group, which was fine with us. The other ten of us were having a wonderful time.

My clumsiness didn't always help situations though. One time, everyone had settled into the tiny communal tent where we ate our evening meals. I was late and rushed over to the tent. As I ran towards it, I slipped and went flying into the tent underneath. Just my luck. I ended up crashing into the two who didn't like me and almost knocked their food over. I was wedged with my head stuck under the tent. Alex, Martyn and my other fellow climbers were in hysterics. The two who didn't like me... not so much!

I feel like mountain climbing was a great training ground for me because it's more than the climb. It's also the socialising, the sleep, the cooking, the camaraderie. I guess looking back now, *Celebrity Big Brother* was a piece of cake compared to that.

My most recent charity climb came at a great time. It was just after Denny had been thrown out of the England rugby team and things were bad between us. I needed the headspace and to be away from him. I didn't know what I was going to do about the whole situation. I could feel my mental health and my husband slipping away, so I headed to Peru. Sometimes just getting away from it all seems the only sensible thing to do.

The first stop was Cusco, in south-east Peru, for a few nights. The city is high above sea level so right away you felt the altitude. We stayed in the city of Cusco first to get our bodies acclimatised to the altitude, which would help us on the climb up the Inca Trail.

The day before the climb, we met the rest of our team members, again mainly Americans. As usual, the climb started and a bond between everyone involved was established. This is always my favourite part. I met a man in his fifties who was a defence attorney from Texas, but originally from Mexico. He had so many tales to tell. I spoke with him a lot. He used to be morbidly obese and lost a heap of weight from hiking and doing these adventures. He had seen some terrible things as a child and I felt I could relate to him. He spoke about his career and had me hooked; I found out the ins and outs of horrible crimes and murders.

I love true crime and so his stories were fascinating to me. I've always wondered what makes a person go over the edge and commit such awful crimes.

Once we completed the Inca Trail, we had a few days to explore. We flew back to the capital of Peru, Lima. Our little English group that travelled together consisted of seven. There was Alex, her boyfriend Tom, Martyn (our leader), a couple named James and Esmé, Phil, a lovely chap in his late sixties who was a bundle of joy, and me. I adored Phil; we all did. He was a proper old-fashioned gentleman, so caring throughout the trip. Once we got to Lima, after the climb, we found out he was a karaoke king! We wanted a few beers to celebrate our climb and went for a walk around

Lima to find a bar. Phil and Alex suggested karaoke and we couldn't find one, so we settled in a bar and started on a few drinks. Phil said he was just going to take a walk up the road and see what else he could find.

After an hour passed, we were tipsy and were starting to worry about Phil. Eventually, he came back after scouting what seemed like the whole capital, and he'd found a karaoke bar that was open. We bundled in and, my God, did we let loose! We were the only group in there other than two women and a man, and we wouldn't let anyone else on stage.

Phil and I did a great rendition of *Barbie Girl* by Aqua, followed by Alex and I going full pelt with *Man! I Feel Like a Woman!* by Shania Twain. By this point we were so drunk.

We sat down for some more drinks, and realised Tom had been missing for a while. A couple of people went out to try to see where he could be, and Martyn found him napping in the toilet! I laughed so much that I fell flat on the floor with my feet still on the stool where I had fallen off backwards. Alex was trying to help me up but ended up falling on top of me. Martyn couldn't breathe because he was laughing so much. When you've done something like climbing a mountain you deserve a night like that! It was one of the most fun nights of my life.

My most recent charity event was the London Landmarks half marathon. As an ambassador of the Guide Dogs' charity I was running to raise money for them. I was there on my own for this one and a little nervous. Luckily, as Alex pointed out, I never really train when I go running; I just have this knack of being able to turn up to a race and do it really fast. Which I did, although I did get a stress fracture in my foot from wearing stupid trainers. One day I'll learn to wear the right footwear! However, I carried on running until the end, completing my first ever half marathon in two hours, three minutes and twenty-nine seconds. I was happy with that, even if I did have to wear a funny air boot for two and a half weeks whilst my foot healed, and had to hobble around everywhere.

There can be a lot of sadness involved in the reasons why people run marathons. Usually it's because they have lost a loved one through illness, or they know someone fighting an illness, etc. When people do these events, they pull together through love.

Love truly is the strongest bond, and when surrounded by people who are doing these events, the energy is wonderful. I get teary every time I run these types of races. Everyone is there cheering you on, lining the streets to keep the runners going, handing out sugar sweets to keep the energy up. It's times like this when I see love and humanity again and it warms my heart.

We see so much sadness everywhere, on the streets and on the news. It damages us when we realise how cruel the world can be, and many people can feel quite cynical when it's rammed down our throats daily. But events like this show us compassion, kindness and love and I can't get enough of it.

Hopefully, next year I'll do the full London Marathon. That's the plan. I want to climb lots more mountains too. I know I'll always have Alex and my mum, and people like Martyn and Lance and the attorney in America with me—and think of all the other special, heroic people I'll meet along the way.

My next adventure is the Five Peaks Challenge. I've heard it's a tough one because you have to climb them one after the other, with very little rest, and within forty-eight hours. This trip is currently postponed due to the Coronavirus but we will be doing the climb when it's safe to do so. Watch this space!

CHAPTER THIRTEEN

Celebrity Big Brother

"Darling, I have an offer here for you. It's for *Celebrity Big Brother*. I've got a contract on my desk."

Me? On Celebrity Big Brother? I was a bit scared, but I was definitely up for it. I thought it would be a unique experience. I mean how many people get to go into the famous *Big Brother* house? Then my agent told me that the theme would be Year of the Woman. Previous series have been so confrontational and scary, but this sounded like something I really wanted to do.

When *Big Brother* first hit our screens, I was about twelve years old, at school in Haslemere. The kids were talking about it so I thought I'd watch some of it myself. I was fascinated by it. I don't know what it was, but it just worked as a brand new TV concept. I'd never seen anything like it. Normal people living in a house that were being filmed twenty-four seven.

I stopped watching *Big Brother* a few years ago, but have always watched the celebrity version. I remember the episode on the day David Bowie died, and Tiffany Pollard told everyone that David was dead but she assumed it was David Gest, who was actually asleep in the next room! That's one of the most incredible things I've ever seen on TV.

One series in particular was really horrible though. People were being so nasty to each other, and it started to get crazy, and I thought, *I don't like the idea of this at all.*

I hoped the Year of the Woman would be less intense. The idea was to celebrate one hundred years of the Women's suffrage in the UK. It was going to teach people about what women have been through in history.

When I put the phone down after talking to my agent, I was ecstatic. It was three weeks before launch night, so straight away I started getting myself prepared. I visualised myself walking down the famous staircase and up into the house. I had my heart set on wearing a gorgeous long red sequin dress, just like Jessica Rabbit, so that's exactly what I got.

Myself and the other contestants were picked up on New Year's Day by a driver and taken to a hotel five minutes from Elstree Studios. Once we arrived at the hotel, our mobile phones were taken from us and that was our communication with the outside world gone, until we left the house when we were evicted or thrown out. It was scary—handing my phone over—but it also felt like a relief.

None of us knew who was going to be starring in this series with us. I thought maybe I would find lots of things out in advance, but I knew nothing. We were kept well-hidden with a chaperone in the hotel rooms. The TV was unplugged so we couldn't see any news. I hadn't brought a book with me as I knew you weren't allowed them in the house. I just sat there, waiting nervously, wondering what it would be like when I was in the *Celebrity Big Brother* house, still not quite believing it was happening.

The contestants had to record video idents for the show, which would be shown in the background and on eviction nights. After I'd done those, I had to eat some food on my own in my hotel room, knowing that the other hotel rooms were full of my future housemates going through the same thing. I was so bored with nothing to do.

Channel 5 provided the chaperones, and I had a really nice one, who put on a podcast for me to listen to as I ate my evening meal before going to bed. I was too scared and excited to sleep.

The next day arrived and it was time to prepare for the live launch. I had a crazy mix of emotions. My nerves were out of control! I kept reminding myself that I had been given an epic, one-in-a-lifetime opportunity.

The press were going crazy, speculating as to who was going into the house, and my name was being thrown about by the tabloids. It was a whirlwind of excitement. It felt weird that if I wasn't in this series, I'd have been at home, eager to watch another series of *Celebrity Big Brother*, wondering who the housemates were going to be. This time one of them was going to be me.

That morning, we were escorted around the hotel with our hoods up so no one could see who we were and tip off the press that they'd seen us. We were taken one at a time, just so we couldn't sneak a glimpse of the other housemates. I'd always assumed that everyone would meet up beforehand, but that doesn't happen. You really do only find things out as soon as you're in the house. There was some final filming for the idents to do, and then after what seemed like hours I headed to the studios, hidden in a blacked-out vehicle. I was taken to my personal dressing room and had to wait there for hair and make-up to come and make me look super glam.

As I sat there, I could hear the studio audience arriving. Shit was getting real! One thing calming my nerves was that my mum and Laureen were in the audience and I'd be able to give them a cuddle before walking across the stage and into the house.

The security man walked me to the stage. He looked at me and said, "You're really nervous, aren't you?"

"I can't get my breath. I don't know what's wrong with me!"

"Don't worry, you're not the only one."

That made me feel a bit better. I was glad other people were also nervous. I could hear the excitement of the crowd from where I was standing. Emma Willis played my introduction tape and I was escorted to the inside stage where I would have my entrance interview, on a small stage where our family were. I could see my mum and Laureen. I hardly remember that interview as I was so nervous.

It was then time to make my way into the house. I ran to the side of the stage and gave Mum and Laureen a huge hug before I started the walk along the stage to the door. The stage was pretty small, but it felt enormous; I was hoping I wouldn't fall down!

The fans of the show were utterly amazing and shouting, "We love you, Jess!" and cheering me along. It was so surreal.

I was officially a *Celebrity Big Brother* contestant. I didn't know how Emma would find me, because sometimes people are funny with glamour models. I hadn't done any glamour modelling for years, but that's how they were defining me on the show. I thought she might think, *Oh, another one*, but I think she really warmed to me and by the time she'd talked to me she'd really calmed me down. Maybe this was all going to be okay.

Mum was really excited. She was glad it was the Year of the Woman because she thought that would give it a bit more substance. I hoped I'd come across well because I knew so many people would be watching and I didn't want to embarrass my family.

The doors opened. I waved to the crowd and started walking down the famous staircase into the lounge area, where I saw Ann Widdecombe, Rachel Johnson, Maggie Oliver, Ashley James, India Willoughby and Malika Haqq.

I'd seen Malika on *Keeping Up with the Kardashians* and I thought, *Oh wow, this is crazy! It's the Kardashians' friend!*

It was incredible to see the house. The house I'd seen so many times on my television! It was even more exciting seeing the iconic diary room. The diary room was famous for always having a different theme and ours was like an iceberg.

It was so daunting to be with a cool bunch of diverse and interesting women. My self-doubt started kicking in, telling me I had no right being there, that I was not up to the standard of these women, but I powered through the evening, terrified inside but putting on a confident mask.

I instantly warmed to Maggie Oliver, the detective inspector who resigned from Greater Manchester Police, claiming the force had failed the victims of the Rochdale sex grooming scandal. She resigned from her job because she felt the force was corrupt, and there were vulnerable girls who weren't being protected. What a brave woman Maggie is.

As a result of her work, nine men were convicted in 2012 and handed jail sentences for various crimes. She was portrayed by Lesley Sharp, one of Britain's best actors, in an incredible BBC drama called *Three Girls*. I was really excited the producers of this series of *Celebrity Big Brother* had booked her. It meant they were allowing real, gritty, interesting characters on to the show. Someone everyone could learn from.

Amanda Barrie was the last to arrive. I was so happy when I saw her. I remember being young and seeing her as Alma on *Coronation Street*, running the café, and even then I really liked her. She was really endearing and likeable, and she was on *Bad Girls* too.

I was worried when I first met Ashley James. Ashley is a model and presenter who was in *Made in Chelsea*. I thought she wouldn't like me—a stupid insecurity. She was lovely to me instantly and I was overjoyed; it was the same with Malika.

At the time we went into the house rumours had been flying around that Kylie Jenner was pregnant and we were all dying to know and eventually got the bottle to ask Malika. She was great with her response though. All she said was, "You'd have to ask Kylie."

The producers did really well to find a good variety of women who had a lot to talk about.

I had a great time meeting those women and finding out about everyone. There were no men for the first few days because of the theme of celebrating all types of women, of all ages and backgrounds. It was so exciting. I was in the *Celebrity Big Brother* house!

The first thing we talked about was the bed situation, and that became the first disagreement. This was between Ann and India. India wanted the single bed at the end which meant Ann would have to share a bed, however Ann had made it clear in her contract she would not be sharing a bed. The single bed India picked had towels on it, with Ann's name on, and India had moved them off. This was our first awkward moment, but we soon settled it. We resolved most things pretty well.

I got on with Rachel Johnson, Boris Johnson's sister. I liked her. To be fair I liked pretty much everyone. My mum said Rachel wrote a really nice article where she said she wanted me to win. I didn't spend as much time with Rachel as I did with Maggie and Amanda.

I felt lucky to be able to have such a variety of conversations. I talked to Ann Widdecombe about politics, and was so happy she was prepared to listen to what I had to say and didn't judge me or look down on me. I don't have the same political views as her, but I really respect her. That's exactly what the point of the series was. Where else would I get to talk to someone like Ann?

The dynamic changed when the boys came in. A part of me wanted it to just continue with the girls, but we'd spent a week together, and it was beginning to get a little dull with such a small group of us, so it was good to have a change. We were ready for something new to happen.

Day-to-day life in the house is incredibly boring. You only get to see an edited hour a day. We would assign people to do the different jobs such as cooking and cleaning, and we were all quite respectful in that way. We all did our bit and took turns.

One thing that stood out on the show was when I had a complete breakdown as I heard Rachel say she hadn't seen me cleaning, but I had been. It was such a tiny thing that I should have laughed at but with trying to adapt to this weird new environment I couldn't help but cry! From the outside it looked totally pathetic.

However, I was actually struggling with so much more in my head. I was still married at the time and I wasn't sure about the state of my marriage on the outside. I was worried about how Denny was coping. I was full of anxiety. I wasn't sleeping well because it's incredibly hard to sleep sharing beds in a huge room with people you had only just met. Sometimes when you were asleep the crew would be building in the sitting room so the doors in the bedrooms would be bolted. It was all a bit overwhelming.

Celebrity Big Brother had this incredible way of waiting until my make-up was off and I was in bed before calling me to the diary room! They did it to Ann too, which ended up becoming a running joke with us! The moment we got into bed—boom!

"This is Big Brother, would Jess please come to the diary room."

I swear those twelve little words haunt me to this day!

I loved the tasks *Celebrity Big Brother* would give us. It was the only real entertainment we had, unless someone was having an argument or a heated discussion. One of my favourites was the foraging task and I got to the final. It was me against Shane Lynch—Boyzone legend! I was so excited with how the crew had turned the outside into a forest. I ran around like a crazy person foraging for the clues they had sent us, and I won! I was over the moon.

Memories that stick out for me from my time on *Celebrity Big Brother* are the things that made me belly laugh. There were so many times this happened. Once, the boys had been gossiping and discussing nominations, which is a big no-no in the house rules. Big Brother punished us by only giving us cold showers. Wayne Sleep was adamant he was getting in the shower, so he came into the bathroom in his little towel, jumped in the shower cubicle and switched the water on. There was silence, then suddenly, loud screams. Wayne was hopping and jumping around, and got out of the shower quicker than lightning. His face was a picture. There were only a few of us in the bathroom and we were in hysterics.

It always seemed to be Wayne Sleep who managed to have me in fits of giggles. My favourite moment with Wayne was when he went to trim his eyebrows but accidentally shaved them off completely. He looked at me and said, "Jess, have I done it okay?"

I couldn't catch my breath through laughter.

I very much believe in signs that guide us through life and I believe if we trust our gut instinct we can really live to our highest self. There have been so many times where I've gone against my gut instinct and things have gone drastically wrong, so it was time to tune in to myself and trust myself.

I practised this one day in the house. I was struggling with my anxiety. I asked for a sign from the universe, just anything to keep me from walking out. I was missing my mum and was worried about her, and it could feel extremely claustrophobic in the house.

I had always seen a robin red breast as a sign of being on the right path. My nan used to have one visit outside her window each day and it became a bit of a thing for us. When she passed away, I always felt her presence when I saw a robin red breast.

This particular day I sat alone in the garden of the *Celebrity Big Brother* house and hid my face under blankets for a little cry. I thought, *Someone please help me get rid of this anxiety so I can enjoy this amazing experience, and give me a sign that my loved ones on the outside world are okay.*

I wiped my eyes and moved the blanket from my face. I couldn't believe what I saw. No birds ever came into the tiny garden because there was netting at the side of the compound. I'd never seen any wildlife come in, but sitting next to me was a robin red breast. I stared at it, completely stunned. It looked at me, did two laps around the garden and then flew out. I had been sent my sign. That moment gave me the strength to get through, and I made it to the final of January 2018's series of *Celebrity Big Brother.*

I will remember those days forever. I met such incredible people. My favourite thing about being on the series was meeting Amanda Barrie. I have so much admiration for her. I love her! She has lived the life I've dreamt of—playing so many amazing characters in the theatre and on award-winning TV shows and films. I was in awe. I was constantly asking her to tell me amazing stories and she had so many. I'd watched her in *Carry on Cleo, Bad Girls* and *Coronation Street*—she was just fantastic and at eighty-two years old was as nimble as I was. I instantly warmed to her.

Amanda said that she didn't have kids and she'd never felt maternal in her life, but she said with me she got the feeling of what it must be like. I thought that was really sweet. I'm so lucky that I met her in such unusual surroundings.

One thing I will always remember Amanda saying to me is, "You've got something kid. Get back into your acting."

That will stay with me forever. It was the boost I so desperately needed from someone who I completely respected in the industry I was so desperate to get back to. I thank Amanda for giving me the confidence I lost all those years ago. It was a turning point for me.

I didn't particularly think about my chances of winning the series, because I knew the other people in the house were much more famous than me. It really didn't make a huge difference who won as it was more about the experience.

I remember the final well. It was the most exciting yet terrifying experience. There were five of us left: me, Courtney Act, Ann Widdicombe, Shane Lynch and Wayne Sleep. We were gathered around the sofas and we could hear the audience outside screaming and chanting. My heart was beating ten to the dozen.

Finally, Emma Willis spoke and announced fifth place. I was certain it was going to be me, but to my surprise it was Wayne. We said our goodbyes then sat back down ready to find out who was leaving next. Fourth place came and this time it was me.

I remember shaking because now I had to go out that door and back to reality. For four weeks and four days I had watched my housemates leave. It was almost like watching them walk off into a spaceship! As people left we could see the open door and bright lights, and we'd hear the loud screams. Our housemates would walk out and the doors would shut behind them, like they had been zapped away to another land.

When I walked out, thankfully it was to a kind audience and cheers. I was dreading walking out to a response like I'd seen in the past, of boos and heckles. I was trembling! I walked out and waved to the cheering crowd and was met by Emma who had a big smile on her face!

Now all I could think about was getting down the stairs without falling down and giving my family a cuddle. I had to take a seat for my final interview with Emma, and as soon as it was over, I ran over to Mum and Laureen who were waiting for me in the family and friends section of the audience, with my manager at the time, Vickie.

Mum had taken full advantage of the free bar and was quite pissed! But nonetheless, it was amazing to have my family there to hug again. I just hoped and prayed I hadn't let them down. I knew they'd have been watching every moment.

I never watched any of that series of *Celebrity Big Brother*. I'd already lived it and I wanted to remember it as it felt in my own memories, rather than seeing if anyone had been saying rude things behind my back, or seeing an edited version of it. I wanted to have nice memories. Someone told me the boys had been nasty about me, but I've never been tempted to see it.

I was recognised a lot in the few weeks after leaving the house. It was crazy. It's died down now; everyone's forgotten about me! But when it was on, it was pretty intense everywhere I went, which was kind of cool, but scary.

After leaving the house I was inundated with companies wanting to work with me on social media collaborations. When coming off reality TV in the era of social media, most people leave the shows with a huge social media following. This gives ample opportunity for people on reality TV to keep making a living and stay relevant.

Many companies picked up on this and were now using these people to endorse their products. It is often cheaper than a TV advert, but also can be a better way of hitting a targeted audience, with the right age range and the right niche, whether it be for fashion, fitness products, books, etc.

When I first came off *Ex on the Beach* and *Celebrity Big Brother*, I had endorsements pouring in. Mainly teeth whiteners and weight-loss shakes. At the time, this was a completely new concept to me. People were actually paying me to just take a picture with this stuff, which I did. What a crazy way to earn money!

The weight-loss tea sounded great to me. I have always been tiny and have never been overweight in my life, but I definitely suffered with a very mild eating disorder growing up. I was always going on diets from a young age. I guess our parents don't realise it, but as a child I would always hear Mum talking about how she needed to diet and hearing that so often rubbed off on me. So eventually it manifested into a minor disorder for me.

When I lived with Nan and Grandad and was still at school, I would often eat dinner then head to the toilet to throw it up. Not one person knew about this.

So when I was being paid to promote these teas once I was older I almost went back to the younger me and started to pick up bad habits, clearly triggering old issues. It didn't even cross my mind that this would be influencing other young girls into eating disorders, as at the time I didn't accept that I had a problem myself. Once I realised my unhealthy relationship with food, I could fix it. It's like with anything really. You have to realise it and admit to yourself there is a problem before you can hit the road to recovery.

Now that I have fixed this problem within myself, I would never again dream of promoting anything on social media that could hurt young, impressionable people. I'm careful with what comes my way, and will only do promotions with companies if I've used the products and tested them first, whether this be gym wear, make-up, protein shakes, etc. Never would I promote something now that promises quick weight loss because I believe it's dangerous, especially as those products basically give you the shits to make you lose weight!

I do feel lucky that I have social media as an extra revenue stream at times, but I've never tried to be or considered myself an influencer. Not that I feel anything bad towards people who use social media to be of influence; I just don't have the passion for it, or a niche to make it a page to influence people.

I've done the occasional fashion post, but in real life I don't have a passion for fashion. I spend most of my life in gym wear! I do paid collaborations when they come in because it definitely helps me, however I'll use the product first and if I don't like it—horrible as it may be to turn down money—I won't promote it now. I find that is the best way to be genuine with products. If you try them and like them, then a collaboration is legit and trustworthy.

Social media is filled with abuse and you often get people moaning or trolling when you do advertising on social media, that's just part and parcel of it. We are in a new era and if this is the new way of advertising, then why should people who have built a following not get involved? It's no different to the television adverts that celebrities endorse and become the face of.

I have a lot of respect for influencers, especially those who ensure that they are positively influencing people's lives. I have friends that do this well and they use their platform to speak up on women's empowerment, new fashion trends and make-up tutorials. My page tends to be more about my everyday life, my acting headshots and showreel clips, or how I motivate myself in the hope that others can take a little bit of that and use it to motivate themselves.

I believe with a big social media following you need to keep a level of responsibility. I have used it wrongly in the past, but I believe I have learned lessons from it. Not everything needs to be a highlight reel to make yourself look perfect. In fact, just being honest about down days can help others greatly.

When I left the *Celebrity Big Brother* house I was terrified of what would happen next, but I knew this was my chance to turn things around in my career and get back to doing what my heart called out for. Amanda Barrie had given me such confidence and I knew I was capable of doing something special with my life.

That week, I went straight to join an adult acting school called ActUpNorth. I had the most wonderful teacher called David Crowley. He really helped me tune into myself and bring out more of my skills. We started working on some material so I could get a good showreel that I could send to casting directors. I put my heart and soul into it. I was back to reading scripts each day and really loving it. All because Amanda Barrie had told me to. I was going to be an actor again.

CHAPTER FOURTEEN

Making Movies

A month after leaving the *Celebrity Big Brother* house, I got a phone call from a production company offering me a role in a new horror film they were making called *The Seven*. It was being produced by Dean Cain, best known for playing Superman alongside Teri Hatcher.

I've always been a *Superman* fan and watched that show when I was a little girl. I was over the moon. It was proof that if I put my mind to something, and went for it, the universe would open up and send me opportunities.

I was sent the script to go over to see if I liked it and if any of the characters jumped out at me as to who I would like to play. I picked the character Ashley because over the course of the movie she gets a few different personalities and it was fun to give that a go.

The film is based in a college that has an awful past and demons lurking within. We were staying in Debden House in Essex. It felt like a university's halls of residence and each of us had our own room. The main seven of us were in our twenties. We had such a great laugh filming; sometimes a few too many and got ourselves in trouble.

One of the characters, played by a fantastic actor called Luke Higgins, was my on-screen love interest. There was one scene when we were on a really tight time schedule. We had already run well over the time schedule and we needed this particular shot nailed ASAP. The scene was Luke and me running, then hiding under a table in the school room. Just as the director, Richard, shouted out, "Action!" Luke let out a huge fart.

Now at this point I was twenty-nine years old and really should have behaved better, but sod it, I'm a kid at heart and growing up is an illusion. I laughed so hard I couldn't catch my breath, which sent the whole crew into a serious laughing meltdown. I had tears streaming down my face, messing up my make-up, but I just couldn't stop.

Luckily, the smudged make-up added to the scene (that's what I managed to convince everyone anyway!). The director tried his hardest to pull us back together and eventually, after delaying everyone an extra twenty minutes, we got the scene done.

That kind of friendship and fun pretty much happened every day we were there. Whilst filming the movie, I was on top of the world. I was exhausted at points from the long hours, but I was *finally* in my element again. I felt like I was in this weird sort of film bubble. Everyone I've spoken to in the film industry says this is how they feel too, but now I've experienced it myself.

I've made three independent movies as a lead or a supporting actress and each time you go away filming, life becomes a little bubble with the cast and crew. You become such a tight group; almost like a temporary family whilst you're away.

Whenever I finish movies, I find it really hard to adapt back to normal life because I miss everything and everyone. It's surprising how well you get to know the character you're playing; you think like them, act like them and become more and more a part of them than you are yourself. Then suddenly the filming is over, the crew go home and everyone goes their separate ways. Real life returns, the character you played disappears into the ether and you have to be yourself again. It's sad! You miss them. I love the whole process so much. I prefer being in a film bubble over everything.

Dean Cain had a scene written in for himself as a cameo in *The Seven*. Originally, I wasn't supposed to be working with him on the movie due to the fact all my scenes were UK based. The film crew had flown over to LA for a mutual friend's wedding that I was also attending, but they were also going to film the scene with Dean. Because we all happened to be in

LA at the same time, the director added a little scene for me so that I was able to act alongside Dean, which was awesome! He is a very talented actor.

After filming, I was going to get a cab back to my hotel in West Hollywood.

Dean stopped me and said, "It's okay, I'll drop you back. I have to head to the CBS TV Studios."

So he drove me back and we had a quick pizza and coffee before he headed off. He told me all about the industry and some very cool Hollywood stories.

Before *The Seven*, I had a small role in a horror flick called *The Tombs: Rise of the Damned*. It was directed by Dan Brownlie. There was a cool cast. Some of the actors were from *EastEnders*, others were from American horror films and it was the first time I felt like I was on a real film set and doing what I loved.

I wasn't one of the main roles. I think I was in about four or five scenes, but it a great experience. I was finally on the path to doing what I loved.

We always did night shoots for filming down in the tombs, deep, deep down below London Bridge. We were the only film crew to have shot a movie down there and, my God, was it scary. We would arrive for hair and make-up at seven in the evening, which would take about two hours. For my character, I needed blood and a pale face. It was so fun getting to dress up. I've found make-up and costume so important for characterisation; I find I can really develop a character better when I'm dressed up as them.

When I first met the cast and crew, I was so nervous. I had these horrible feelings that I wasn't good enough to be there. I thought people would be looking down on me because I'd done reality TV and I hated that I let my self-doubts get to me. I had such a great cast and crew and we got on so well, so I was able to fight through the negative feelings and was pleased with my performance.

Before long I was loving every minute of filming. Well, almost every minute. . . I was absolutely terrified filming down in the tombs!

During the day, when it's a tourist attraction, it's scary enough, so imagine when it's just a film crew and actors in the middle of the night until seven o'clock in the morning. I was too scared to even go to the toilet by myself! There were so many creepy corridors and weird noises down there that I was on edge the whole time and would literally run from the make-up room to the set, in case a ghost got hold of me or something jumped out of the darkness.

One time, I was desperate to go to the toilet and all the runners (which are the people who help out on film sets working their way up the ranks) were busy so I had to go alone. I locked the door and sat down and creepy clown music started to play. I'd been told the attraction's music and things that make you jump on the tour during the day would be turned off, and it had been. So how on earth was this music playing?

I'd watched far too many scary movies to be dealing with this. Being alone on the toilet is up there with one of the most vulnerable places to be if a killer is lurking outside. Knowing no one was anywhere nearby to save me, I kept visualising some killer clown bursting through the toilet door, and I wouldn't be able to do a hell of a lot! Of course, nothing actually happened. I have such an overactive imagination sometimes.

Even though I only had a few days of filming on *The Tombs*, I loved being part of the gang. It gave me a kick to get up and keep going. It's addictive being surrounded by film crews and people passionate about making films. It also got me back on the map, and soon enough *The Seven* movie came up. I still to this day haven't seen *The Tombs* as it has only had a US release, which is super annoying as it was my first proper role since school.

After *The Seven* wrapped up, a new script was sent to me from the makers of the film, so I must have done a pretty good job. I looked through it and I realised I would be playing the lead! It was a sci-fi film called *RIA*. I was over the moon. I'd be playing the movie's namesake.

The cast was huge: Luke Goss, from the band Bros; Dean Cain was on board again as one of the supporting actors; Charlie Clapham from *Hollyoaks*; former Pussycat Doll Kimberly Wyatt; Mark Holden, who has been in films such as *Captain Phillips*; and Leon Ockenden from *Mr*

Selfridge. Things were getting bigger and I was beside myself with excitement. To be beside these actors was a real honour, and whereas I'd been nervous in previous roles, I wanted to prove to everyone I was a proper actor now. This was the biggest role of my life.

Playing Ria was hard because (without giving the entire plot away!) I had to forget how to play someone based on emotions, which is the way a lot of my teachers taught me to act. Generally, you tap into different emotions and experiences you've had and work them into any character you're playing. As soon as you watch the film, you'll realise why I was so desperate to get the role and why it was something unusual.

The first day with Luke Goss scared the life out of me. He's such a talented actor. I'd seen him in *Hellboy* and other big movies. I knew this was where I could grow. The best thing about working on films is working with great actors. Luke helped me emerge out of myself and become better and more confident (thanks, Luke!). He was an amazing presence and was always happy to help me with tips and ideas. Having someone like him co-starring with you is fantastic. It automatically brought out a better performance in me.

One day, Luke said he thought I was really talented. Jeez, I was so relieved! It meant a lot to me. Having crippling self-doubt, someone like Luke telling me I was doing a good job helped more than you can imagine.

Like all jobs, being an actor is about teamwork, and if the person you're alongside supports and believes in you, it makes life so much easier. I really hope I get to work with Luke Goss again and that one day I'm that established actor and can help the new, nervous actor working with me.

I want to be the one to say, "You're brilliant! Keep going. You're so talented. Please never give up!"

Far too often I've let self-doubt and fear stop me from progressing but now, finally, that has stopped. If I want something, by hell I'm going for it! It's a tough thing to do, pushing through self-doubt and fear, but the more you do it, the less it rears its ugly head. We can never grow or learn from inside our own comfort zones. So, keep pushing for your dream! We all have them. Fight for it!

There were so many funny moments when filming *RIA*. There were a lot of the same crew members from when we filmed *The Seven* so it was as if the family had reunited. Our sound guy, Paul, was one of my favourite people to work with. He was so funny, and often misunderstood in his approach to work. He is a very skilled sound guy, but when things are not going to plan he could get in a right strop, but this always made us laugh our socks off. He would say the silliest things and we would be in hysterics. He made the days so much more fun.

One day, he wanted Buffalo wings for lunch, so our producer Amar started a dare. This was on an easy day of filming and I was the only actor on set. We said to Paul that if he spent the next three hours doing his job in his underpants, he would get his Buffalo wings. We didn't really think he'd go along with it, but he stripped off! We were beside ourselves with laughter. To make it even funnier, we hid his clothes in the freezer, so when it was time for him to get dressed, his jeans and T-shirt were literally frozen stiff. I made friends for life from working with that film crew.

Currently, whilst writing this book, we are waiting for news on the release of *RIA*, and to which platforms you can view it on. For a small budget independent film I think we did a great job! I've seen the rough cut of the movie and I'm really proud of it. Because of Coronavirus everything is slightly up in the air. The movie release has been affected by this, but I'm hopeful soon enough you'll be able to see it.

I'm absolutely in my element when I'm making movies. I know I've got a long way to go, but I get so much joy out of every moment, from when I first get to read the script to actually being on set. I'm enjoying learning the trade and becoming better at what I do. I know I'll succeed.

There are lots of people who like to tear you down or be cynical or unkind, but if you're confident within yourself no one can touch you. People only ever do it out of jealousy because you're achieving something they're not. They try to discredit you and make out you're not worthy of your success. When this happens, please know you're doing something right and you're on the right path. The success of others scares people who haven't pushed hard enough to get it themselves. They're the people who don't work hard enough, or have allowed fear to stop them from pushing on to achieve what they want in life.

My advice is always to keep going. You'll get there, my friend!

CHAPTER FIFTEEN

Spirituality

I have always had an overactive brain; it goes in-depth with everything. What comes after death? How big is the universe? Does it ever stop? As humans, we only know a beginning and an end. What happens at the end of the universe? Is there an end of the universe? Would we just hit a black, dark wall, caging us in? How vast the universe could be is actually quite a daunting thought.

I was at my mum's house in Haslemere one weekend. Nan had recently passed away and I was lying in her room, scrolling through Instagram, looking for a new book to read. I've always been a bookworm and I was looking up books on self-progression.

I stumbled across a girl's profile and she was talking about a book by Paulo Coelho called *The Alchemist*. Many of you may have heard of it, or even read it. I truly believe this book was the beginning of change for my entire life. For my growth, my confidence and simply putting my life back on the right course.

Sometimes the world seems to give us little things, and these little things add up and become big things. It's no coincidence. It's signs showing us we're moving in the right direction.

I started meditating, collecting a few healing crystals and finding new books about spirituality. I would do this periodically. However, when I found out my husband cheated, I really turned to it. I think the universe really had my back there. I was so lost when Denny cheated and my marriage was coming to an end. I didn't know where to turn. Having some knowledge of meditation and controlling my thoughts let me jump into this practice and got me through the worst times of my life.

I always make sure I have a goals and gratitude book to hand. I simply get a cute notepad and when I wake up, I write down what I'd like to achieve that day. That could be work related or even something such as 'to treat everyone with love today and let no outside situation disturb my inner peace and love.'

That sounds easy, right? But it can be a hard thing to do. It's where you learn to see why someone behaves in a certain manner, rather than be defensive. It's to understand and know that if someone is mean or aggressive, it's not your fault and you can just hope their day gets better. That way, they cannot take away your inner peace because you refuse to get flustered or upset when they behave in that manner. Their negativity doesn't filter into your day and you can continue having a wonderful day.

I admit this can be hard with loved ones, and I still have to practise this all the time. But the more you practise kindness and looking after your inner happiness, the easier it gets.

At the end of my day, when I'm getting into bed, I'll write my gratitude list for the day. I'll write down anything I'm proud of, or anything that made me smile. Basically, any little or big thing that made my day more positive. Even if you have to find something tiny, it helps you to start seeing the good in the day rather than focusing on anything bad. I especially like doing this before I sleep because it fills me up with happiness, I fall asleep in a good mood, so by the morning I'm totally refreshed.

In the past when I found myself in depression and falling asleep to tears, I realised I would get myself in such a dark hole because I was going to bed sad and waking up still sad—it was a snowball effect. Writing in my gratitude book before bed stops that process and just does it in reverse.

I find the moon cycles fascinating too. If the movement of the moon is what causes the tides to rise and fall, it only makes sense that our bodies react to it also. As humans we are made up of about 60% water. I definitely know that my body and behaviour are different around the time of the full moon. I'm usually a bit more wired or on edge, and now that I follow the moon cycle I know when I'll feel like that, so I find it easier to deal with my emotions.

The average female menstrual cycle is twenty-eight days, which is also the same length of time as the moon cycle, and I think that just shows how connected we are to this planet.

I often meditate with my healing crystals because I'm a firm believer in energy transfer. I often get mocked for my belief in crystal healing, and I know it's not for everyone but it helps me. I believe certain crystals had a massive role in my healing process. I felt calmer and found it easier to deal with my emotions when I had my crystals near me, or if I meditated with them in my hands. If that makes me feel better, then I'll continue to do so.

When we're young, we develop certain beliefs about ourselves. We pick up little things from our environment, our parents, our peers, the media, etc. Whether we're too short, too tall, too fat, too thin. Then we go about our lives trying to change these things. I've been the worst at this. I had beautiful long curly hair growing up and my first love at seventeen was still crazy about his ex, who was pretty and blonde, so I bleached my whole head blonde to make him fancy me more. If I looked like her, maybe he would be with me. It's insane, isn't it?

It has taken me thirty years to realise that what's on the outside doesn't matter one tiny bit if the inside isn't in a good place. I would attract cheaters and liars and people who didn't see my worth, then wonder why it would never work out. Now I see it was because I had no self-worth or self-love, plain and simple. How could I expect anyone else to love me if I couldn't love myself?

That's why my spirituality is so important to me. It teaches me to give myself time out, to love myself. It shows me that you don't have to please everyone else to your own detriment; you can say no if something doesn't feel right.

I used to get nervous if a man flirted with me because I didn't want to be rude and say no! I feel sad for the younger me, but I'm so in love with me now. It was growth that I had to go through, and I'm so proud of myself for going through it.

I make a conscious choice every day to meditate. I see it like this: you have a shower to wash yourself with each day, to clear the dirt, so meditation is like washing the dirt out of your mind and clearing yourself to get the most from a new day.

My spirituality isn't simply a thing I decided to do one day and suddenly I was happy. It doesn't work like that. I had to drag out old, painful emotions that I'd hidden away. I let them out of my body to let myself heal.

To heal, you need to visit these darker emotions and become at peace with them. I have a long, long journey still ahead of me with my healing and spirituality. In fact, it will never stop. I hope to continue with these habits of meditating throughout my life.

If I get a negative feeling of sadness, jealousy or rage, I can control them now. I can go and meditate on them, knowing how to get rid of them. I can feel them without hurting anyone else in the wake of them. These feelings crop up in all of us and never lead to any positive outcome. So I like to get rid of them as quickly as possible.

I love Gabby Bernstein's fantastic books. My favourites are *Spirit Junkie* and *The Universe Has Your Back*. I also love *Judgement Detox* because it goes into how we judge others and ourselves, which leads us to horrid feelings such as shame. I really didn't realise how much we judge ourselves and others until I read this and made a conscious choice to stop. I can assure you, once you stop doing it and catch yourself, a shift happens. I realised what I judged in others I saw in myself. I would put up a hard shell to protect myself from my own judgements. I learnt to forgive myself for not treating myself right and that's when the journey of self-love kicked in.

One thing I would really love to stress to people is to never lose your inner child. Be silly. Have fun. Because society tells us to grow up, we get so serious. But without my sense of silliness and fun, I stopped laughing and became so depressed. By finding myself again throughout this whole process, I stopped caring what people thought.

I have a crazy obsession with *Harry Potter*. I used to keep that to myself. Not now! I tweet and Instagram with pride. Sharing my trips to the *Harry Potter* Studio Tour or the *Harry Potter* section in Universal Studios in LA. I even re-read the books nearly every year. It brings me so much joy and out comes my inner child. We need to hold on to the things that are good for our soul and our bodies. I promise it makes the world of difference.

If I come across someone who has really negative energy and I worry it may bring me down, I often visualise an imaginary bubble around me and that the negativity cannot touch me. Often, when I'm around people like this, my happy energy rubs off on the other person, just through me being kind and understanding towards them, and they leave feeling better.

Sometimes, if someone is having a bad day and their energy is low, a simple smile can make them feel better. One thing I think is important is to stop finding offence in what people say. If someone calls us ugly or stupid, or even something not as direct as that, we can often get defensive and offended, which can lead to an argument. I've learnt not to take offence from people saying nasty things to me. It shows a problem with them.

If I see road rage directed towards me, I just smile. This wasn't always the case. I used to get so frustrated in the car if people weren't driving how I thought they should be, or holding up traffic, but now instead of losing my temper and being rude, I think, How would I like someone to treat me in this situation, and what if the person in the car was my grandparents, my niece or nephew, or Mum or Dad? That will stop me from getting cross with them because I'd hate the thought of someone being mean to my loved ones. Plus, even if we are in a rush, getting worked up and breaking the law by speeding isn't going to make much of a difference.

I've learned a clear difference between what we deem to be someone's fault and what is our own responsibility: when we blame someone for something that's happened in our lives, we often say things like "It's his fault I'm in this situation" or "It's her fault my heart is broken" and so on. This is living in victim mode, and once in victim mode you hit a block. Let me explain. It might well be someone's fault for what they made you feel, but it's your responsibility to fix your own life. No matter what anyone has done to you, if you don't take ownership of your own life, you'll be stuck. Someone else may have broken something, but it's not their responsibility to fix you. It's yours and yours alone.

I read a lot of books by Dr Wayne Dyer. I thoroughly recommend them. I often download them on my Audible App and listen to them whilst driving. My favourite quote of his is, *'When you change the way you look at things, the things you look at change.'* It's such a beautiful quote, and so very accurate.

If your inner world is beautiful, your outer world will reflect that. The world around you picks up on your energy. Think of it like this: if you're in an office and your boss walks in in a foul mood and is snappy and rude to everyone, suddenly everyone in the office feels that energy and their day might be dampened, yet if the boss came in happy and kind, the energy of the room would be completely different. So always have a good energy and good vibes will be sure to follow you around. Keeping a beautiful inside makes your outer world beautiful too!

So go with the flow. Take ownership and responsibility of your own life. Everything happens for a reason. Take the hard times as lessons. Just enjoy each and every moment, because sometimes if we take just a little time to notice it, we can see that life really is beautiful. I've learnt that despite all the hardships I've experienced, there's always a silver lining.

BONUS CHAPTER

Guide Dog Stories

When I was a child, I remember seeing a blind man with a guide dog. My mum would tell me that they were specially trained dogs doing very important work. At this point not one person on earth thought Mum would ever have guide dogs of her own.

I thought then about how they must be a special kind of dog, with some form of magical brains—how could a dog take someone around and keep them safe? I never really gave it much more thought until all those years later, when Mum received her first dog.

What amazed me was the effort, time and dedication that went into every single guide dog to ensure they became the amazing life-changers that they really are. I was lucky enough after filming *Celebrity Big Brother* to take a tour around the National Breeding Centre in Leamington Spa, where I was shown the cute little puppies that would go on to become trained guide dogs. It was the best day ever. I was given a full tour of the centre and the highlight was lying down whilst a load of puppies ran over me in the playpen.

I was so intrigued to find out how the dogs went from being playful little puppies to learning that when they had their work uniform on (the guide dog harness), they needed to turn into serious workers.

Becoming an ambassador for Guide Dogs was such a great honour. It's something I'm so passionate about and it meant I could have much more involvement with the charity and help spread the word. I have taken part in many half marathons to raise as much money as possible and hopefully soon I'll get to run the full marathon for them.

I went to visit the Guide Dogs' headquarters not so long ago to have a chat with Tom Wright, the charity's CEO, who gave me an amazing insight into their history and explained how much it costs to keep everything running. This only gave me more determination to help. I'd seen first-hand how much a guide dog changed my mum's life, so I wanted to help in any way possible so that more people with sight loss can get the freedom they deserve with one of these life-changing animals.

I was able to sit down with the charity and ask questions about the amazing work that goes on behind the scenes with each and every guide dog. I would love to share the answers with you.

ME: First of all, I'd like to understand how the puppies are selected. Since the dogs are carefully bred, what are you looking for in the parents of new litters?

TOM: The extensive research that goes into planning every mating enables the breeding programme managers to highlight which pups, once born, will be of most interest to them as potential breeders in the future. Any successful breeding programme must aim to add new breeding animals of at least the same, if not greater quality, than their parents. We monitor all pups marked as potential breeding stock throughout the puppy-walking phase and assess littermates too, via comprehensive reports from Dog Care and Welfare and the puppy-walking supervisors.

We also have a dedicated member of the team at the Breeding Centre whose role it is to co-ordinate this important work. Good candidates for breeding are practically assessed at eight months of age. Those deemed suitable go on to have further health checks (hip, shoulder and elbow x-rays; eye tests; and so on) and then they have a final assessment before hopefully being accepted onto the breeding programme at twelve months of age. The final assessments take place at the Breeding Centre.

Once accepted onto the breeding programme, the stud or bitch is placed with an appropriate volunteer who has already received training in how to look after their new dog and advice on what to expect in the coming weeks, months and years. However, acceptance is not a guarantee of use, and each newly accepted dog will be reviewed again at eighteen months to ensure it is still of the right quality in both temperamental and health terms. This check is carried out within a regular monthly breed review meeting which is a formalised gathering of breeding management, the chief veterinary consultant, and the national dog care and welfare manager.

ME: When do the selected guide dog puppies leave the Breeding Centre and what is the process for them once they leave?

TOM: Wherever possible our puppies are born in our volunteer brood bitches' homes, where they stay until they're about seven weeks old. Then they move to the National Breeding Centre. They normally stay there for about a week or two to have their injections and final check-ups before they go out on their puppy walks. They stay with their puppy walkers, learning basic skills and commands and becoming familiar with everyday sights, sounds and situations. They stay with the puppy walkers until they're about fourteen months old.

Then they go on to the next stage of their training for a couple of months, living with boarders, before going into advanced training and being matched with their guide dog owner at about twenty months old. They normally work until they're about nine or ten, when they'll enjoy a well-earned retirement!

ME: Once they are fully trained guide dogs, how are they matched to their person? I know my mum had her trainer visit her for a month or so and they would learn their routes together until they passed safety tests together.

TOM: During the training of the dogs, we are constantly assessing their temperament and behaviours and thinking of the type of person we could match the dog to.

The matching process is one of the most critical stages; if we don't get the right match, the partnership is unlikely to succeed. Every person and dog is an individual so there are many different aspects to consider when looking for the best match. Some of the key things we consider are:

- Speed: each dog and person will have their own natural walking speed.
- Working environments: some dogs would thrive in a busy city like London; others would become overwhelmed but would do well in suburban or rural environments.
- Workload: some dogs could work all day whereas others would be more content with a trip to the local shops.
- Family circumstances.
- Long-term aspirations of the service user.
- Personal preferences: breed and so on.

When we have identified a potential match on paper, we would normally go and visit the service user to talk with them about the dog and introduce them to each other. If that goes well, we do a harness walk to see if they are compatible. If they are, we will often place the dog with the service user overnight so that they can observe the social behaviour, as this forms the largest part of their time together.

If we agree it's a good match, we will confirm how and when the partnership will commence training. Training of the partnership is called Creating New Partnerships (CNP) and takes place over a minimum of five weeks, but it's sometimes longer. It's a bit like learning to drive a car in that you're taught the basics of working safely together and you receive more independence as the partnership develops. The service user is also taught how to care for and about the welfare of their dog.

When we are satisfied that the partnership is safe and effective, the service user and a guide dog representative will sign an agreement and the partnership is then qualified to work independently. The partnership will continue to build on their confidence and knowledge together with intermittent support from the guide dog mobility instructor.

ME: I know how important raising money is to keep the charity running. There are always events to take part in, and people are able to sponsor a puppy. Can you tell us any more about how much it costs to train up a single guide dog and the expenses required for their amazing work to continue?

TOM: In 2018, it cost around £63,000 to breed, train and support a guide dog from birth to retirement. However, the cost of a guide dog is impacted not just by the cost of breeding and training, but also the cost of our support functions over an average of seven years, as well as external support such as food and vets' bills.

In 2018, the cost of a guide dog was broken down as follows:

- Breeding and puppy walking costs—£10,100
- Costs to breed and train, and partnership costs—£48,100
- Ongoing support—£2,500

A guide dog owner may have as many as eight guide dogs in their lifetime, bringing the total cost to around £500,000.

How we spend your money

- £5 can support a working guide dog for a day.
- £25 can buy a white harness, the iconic symbol of a fully qualified guide dog.
- £95 can buy a Training School Kit for a guide dog trainer who teaches pups the specialist skills they will need to become a qualified guide dog.
- £140 can buy a Starter Kit for a new guide dog owner, containing everything they need to start a life with their guide dog.

As you can see, it is an expensive and prolonged process, with so much work being put into each and every guide dog and their owner and the ongoing support for the partnership.

I very much enjoyed my trips to the National Breeding Centre and Guide Dogs' HQ. One thing I always found so wonderful was the love that everyone who works there has for these amazing life-changing dogs.

CEO Tom Wright had his beautiful dog, Dolly, with him during our interview. Dolly is a black Labrador who will be one of the possible breeding stock, becoming Mum to some amazing puppies who may go on to become guide dogs. It was clear to see how much the charity meant to Tom and how much he adored Dolly, and I must say, she was adorable.

ME: Can you tell me about the history of the Guide Dogs' charity?

TOM: The principle of guide dogs dates back to the First World War, if not earlier. There's a famous sculpture in Manchester: one hand on top of another. It's said there was a German doctor who had a German shepherd and he saw soldiers whose vision had been affected by gas, and his German shepherd started to act as a guide to them. You could say that was the first-ever guide dog.

In 1929, one of the American guide dog schools was formed. In 1931, we opened ours here in the UK, and then in 1933 in the Netherlands. So, we are the second oldest guide dog school in the world. The dogs were rehomed or retrained dogs. Eventually people started going to Crufts and getting specialist breeders. It took a while until we were breeding our own specialist dogs. We're coming up to our ninetieth birthday soon. Of all the guide dog charities in the world, we are the largest. No other guide dog school is on our scale. America has twelve large, well-established guide dog schools and in Australia there are seven. Here, it's just us.

ME: How important are the volunteers for the charity?

TOM: We employ 1,500 people in the UK and we have 16,000 volunteers. If we paid the volunteers that would be £150 million. Effectively, our volunteers are worth £150 million to us; they're critical to the whole model. They are involved to such a high level—it's a twenty-four-hour, seven-days-a-week commitment.

If you're a specialist breeder, like I am, you'll see three or four litters through your house. The average litter size is eight per dog. You might be familiar with the term 'whelping.' That's the word we use for when dogs give birth. Puppies are born in the volunteers' homes, not in a specialist place.

We have breeding experts. They're like dog midwives. They're on call twenty-four seven. They'll come and support you in your home through what can be a long labour time period. Every volunteer has a relationship with their local vet's to help support them. The majority of puppies are born without specialist help. Just naturally in the puppies' home. Sometimes we bring dogs here for whelping at the National Breeding Centre.

Another volunteer role is a stunt dog holder. They come here to the Breeding Centre in the mating room. It's not exactly what you might expect—there's no music playing, candles or Barry White. But maybe we'll introduce that one day! Then there's puppy walking as well.

"We're lucky to have so many incredible people involved. Two sisters in Scotland walked ninety puppies between the two of them. We have boarding volunteers too. Voluntary work can mirror your lifestyle. Many people are working couples; they pick up a puppy on the way home on a Friday night and look after it over the weekend. Lots of couples say they want a dog but can't because of work, so this is perfect for them. You can take your puppy to work with you, providing the work environment is suitable and the necessary provisions are made for the puppy.

ME: What commands does each dog learn? I find them impressive.

TOM: A guide dog is trained to do thirty-six tasks. Basic life skills. One of those skills is to just enable them to behave like a normal dog when they're not working. We're quite progressive here about using positive reinforcement to train our dogs. We like to allow free running. Some guide dog organisations are against this, because a guide dog owner would be unlikely to ever allow the dog to run free, but we encourage that in their development. Our dogs seem to appreciate that when they're on the harness they're working, and when they're off the leash they're running around and rolling around and they have fun still.

If a dog is comfortable in its surroundings, it will make better decisions. We don't want robotic dogs. It takes six months to fully build up that bond and intuition and confidence. You can tune into your dog and realise it's telling you something. This allows you to live your life more fully and navigate it with more confidence. Hopefully, it's the other way round too.

My mum's guide dogs are a complete reflection of what he'd just told me.

They're incredible to watch. They have fun and act like normal dogs and live life to the full, but as soon as the harness is on they become workers. It really is amazing to see.

From the tours I've been so lucky to go on around the National Breeding Centre—and of course getting to meet everyone at Guide Dogs' HQ—I'm aware of the other services the Guide Dogs' charity has to offer, such as the buddy dog programme.

ME: Can you tell me a bit more about the buddy dog programme?

TOM: There are buddy dogs for blind or partially sighted children who aren't old enough to have a guide dog, although we have lowered the age from eighteen to twelve. Buddy dogs support children in schools and are there to help a child increase their physical activity, build confidence, create better relationships with others, and develop a sense of fun and trust. They are a great way to teach the children the responsibility for caring for a dog. However, they are not a guide dog. We are expanding this service to adults. When you're older, a companion dog might be a bit more appropriate than a guide dog. Or if you have sufficient sight you may not need all the services provided by a guide dog and a companion dog could be just as good. That means guide dogs can be more widely available."

After my meeting with Tom, I was shown to the back of the Guide Dogs' HQ to another smaller building. There was a special room where they make large-print books for children with visual impairments. These books are made in different font sizes specific to the child's needs. To my ultimate joy (being a massive *Harry Potter* fan), I noticed a huge wall stacked up with really large *Harry Potter* books. This is just another great service from the charity.

I came away from my day at Guide Dogs' HQ with such pride. I am forever grateful I have the honour of being an ambassador for the charity and for the work they continue to do. Seeing people all over the country have their lives changed for the better by these amazing people is one of the most rewarding things I could ever ask to be a part of.

If you want to know more about becoming a volunteer for the charity or the sponsor of a puppy programme, more information can be found at www.guidedogs.org.uk.

About the Author

Jess Impiazzi was born on March 9th 1989 and during school years went on to train as a performer at the Italia Conti Academy of Theatre arts. Later gaining a full scholarship into the college.

Best known for her appearances on MTV's *Ex on the Beach*, *Celebrity Big Brother*, and guest appearances on *Loose Women* and Channel 4's *The Wright Stuff*. Alongside her movies, *The Tombs*, *The Seven* and *RIA* where she took her first female lead roll alongside actors such as Luke Goss and Dean Cain.

Jess is an avid ambassador to The Guide Dogs for the Blind charity after her mother lost her eyesight when Jess was in her late teens. She has lobbied Parliament with the charity.

With a keen fitness and self-development attitude, she is a regular in the gym, and on self-development courses. After finding a new lease of life from changing her lifestyle and thoughts, she wanted to help others do the same and document her processes as to how it came about. This is how *Silver Linings* was born.